BLOOMING
into CONSCIOUSNESS

THE EVOLUTION OF YOUR SOUL

Lynn Hooper

BALBOA.
PRESS

A DIVISION OF HAY HOUSE

Balboa Press books may be ordered through booksellers or by contacting:

Balboa Press
A Division of Hay House
1663 Liberty Drive
Bloomington, IN 47403
www.balboapress.com
1 (877) 407-4847

Because of the dynamic nature of the Internet, any web addresses or
links contained in this book may have changed since publication and
may no longer be valid. The views expressed in this work are solely those
of the author and do not necessarily reflect the views of the publisher,
and the publisher hereby disclaims any responsibility for them.

The author of this book does not dispense medical advice or prescribe
the use of any technique as a form of treatment for physical, emotional,
or medical problems without the advice of a physician, either directly
or indirectly. The intent of the author is only to offer information
of a general nature to help you in your quest for emotional and
spiritual well-being. In the event you use any of the information in
this book for yourself, which is your constitutional right, the author
and the publisher assume no responsibility for your actions.

Any people depicted in stock imagery provided by Thinkstock are
models, and such images are being used for illustrative purposes only.

Scripture taken from the King James Version of the Bible.

Certain stock imagery © Thinkstock.

Print information available on the last page.

ISBN: 978-1-5043-6553-6 (sc)
ISBN: 978-1-5043-6552-9 (e)

Balboa Press rev. date: 12/26/2017

A guide to understanding the choices you made in the spiritual realm before you came here and how they affect your life now

There is an old saying: No man is your enemy, no man is your friend, every man is your teacher.

– Florence Scovel Shinn

This Book Explores

- how choices you made in the spirit world are affecting your life now;
- how to become consciously aware of your eternal existence;
- the role angels play in our lives;
- how our loved ones are healed when they pass over to spirit;
- how children grow up in the spirit world;
- how we live in multidimensional lives;
- tuning in to your inner guidance and intuition;
- learning to channel your guides.

Contents

Preface

I had no idea I was writing *Blooming into Consciousness* when I first put pen to paper a few years ago. My life was difficult, and I remember being awake at night, my mind constantly thinking of the struggles I was going through, and not being able to sleep because of them. It was distressing for me, and I would wake up the next day, tired and restless. I decided I couldn't carry on the way I was going, and through sheer desperation, I decided that if I was awake anyway, I might as well take a pen and pad with me and write out what was troubling me to try and release it by asking the spirit world for help and guidance with what was going on in my life at that time.

I struggled at first, not knowing how to start, but then I thought, I go to a spiritualist church; I give readings to people just through a sense of knowing, so where am I getting this information I am giving out to others? How can I get this information to help myself?

I remembered sitting for years in development circles and in meditation, feeling such peace and seeing and hearing such beautiful things that I decided I would ask if there really was anyone there in spirit and, if there was, to please start to communicate with me as I wrote on my pad. At first I was all over the place and would write words and sentences that didn't make any sense. I kept asking questions, and then, after a couple of attempts, I noticed that I seemed to be answering my own questions. Then I doubted the validity of the spirit connection and thought, I am just making this up. Even so, I kept writing, because it was starting to help me feel better.

After a few weeks of doing this exercise every night, I noticed I was looking forward to my writing and the communication, as it was soothing. I would always start with the same words: "Namaste. Welcome, my child." It was as though I was being calmed down and brought into a vibrational energy of peace.

Some days I was stressed and felt so exhausted I would scribble erratically on the paper or draw shapes to just relax enough to allow the word to flow. Eventually I would start to question every answer that I wrote, and always I was given an answer that I knew did not come from me, as the tone and words used were different from how I would normally speak. For example; in answer to a question I had about ego, this was my guide's answer:

> *Many seek the light; the knowledge it has,*
> *but many seek in the wrong corridors. The*
> *hallways of vanity and greed do not belong*
> *amongst the wealth of spirit.*

I would never have written in that style or tone. I accepted that it was not my thoughts that were being conveyed even though I was doing the writing!

I practised this writing exercise every evening for several years, and the unconditional support and love from the spirit world was overwhelming. It kept me going during some of the most difficult days of my life. In the same years that I was writing, I was also going out and practising my mediumship, but I lacked confidence in my abilities. I would talk to spirit about how badly I felt I was doing, and I was encouraged and inspired to keep going when I wanted to give up.

Eventually, as I progressed, my writing followed more spiritual questions in relation to the people I was meeting and giving readings to, and I started to ask what the point was of all the struggles we all seemed to be going through. Then I couldn't seem to stop the flow of writing, and I wrote at high speed over several days. This is now written for you to read also over the chapters of this book.

You might notice that the writing seems a little formal at times, but I realised that what I had done was a spiritual term called *channelling*, where you allow an energy or energies to flow though you, speaking the words you receive out loud or writing them down. As I had practised this type of writing over several years, I was able to write down the channelled words that came directly from spirit.

I am using the term *spirit* to describe a collective energy in non-physical form that is able to communicate with me via my thoughts, imagination, and feelings, and also physically through their ability to move into my physical body and take over my movements, gestures, and speech. There are two clear ways to channel spirit.

Unconscious Channel

If you are an unconscious channel it will be like falling asleep. In a deep meditative state your conscious awareness disappears, and you are unaware of your guides message or words as they work though you. When you are an unconscious channel, you do not remember anything your guides have said when you come back into your conscious mind.

Conscious Channel

If you are a conscious channel, you will be able to remember or be aware of some of your guide's words or messages but not all of them.

I am now a full-time psychic medium, counsellor, and life coach, and I find myself giving the same answers to questions I am repeatedly asked, such as the following:

- Why are these bad things always happening to me?
- Is the spirit world real?
- Do our loved ones and angels really watch over us?
- What happens to our loved ones when they pass over?

And there were so many more questions that I found myself saying to clients, "I really need to write this in a book so everyone can read about these questions and answers." The questions may vary a little from person to person depending on their experiences, but the answers on the whole do not change. For instance, questions I have been asked many times about children include the following:

- Will my child go to spirit even though I aborted them on the physical earth plane?
- Why did my child get taken from me and pass at such a young age?
- How is it possible that an innocent child could die from such a terrible disease?

Although these heartbreaking questions are worded differently depending on the personal experience, the answer is much the same.

We choose the family we are born into. We choose our parents, siblings, and particular friends we share throughout our lives. The child that has been aborted agreed with you before you both incarnated that each of you would give each other the experience. The child agreed that he or she would go back home, and you agreed to give the child the experience.

The child also agreed with you to give you the experience of his or her return home. Your reasons for doing so will be known to both of you before you incarnated into the physical. You also understood from the broader spiritual perspective that you are eternal and you would be reunited upon each of your return home to spirit where you would both review your experiences that had been shared with each other.

This experience sharing is what you have agreed, whether a child is aborted or has passed from a disease or even an accident. These are the major life decisions that you have chosen, but you also knew that you would not be aware of those decisions once you came into the physical earthly life. Our reasons for choosing these experiences are to expand our consciousnesses in the physical and evolve our souls, individually, and as a collective part of humanity.

I sat for many months pondering how to start the book, when I realised that I had already written or channelled a large part of the work, and all I needed to do was add the extra questions that had arisen afterwards. That is how this book came into being to help ease suffering, to explain it is OK to forgive ourselves, and to understand we choose our experiences, family, and difficulties here—not because we want to suffer but because we wish to experience certain conditions that will help us grow or evolve our own unique souls. Armed with that knowledge, we will have a fresh, inspired approach to how we view our lives and realise how quickly we can ease our suffering and live more fulfilled and happy lives as a result of this knowledge.

I hope that some of you may find as much comfort from the knowledge and love shared from the spirit world as I did, and still do, and that you gain insight and peace within the pages of this book that help ease you along each day on your own spiritual journey.

Namaste.

Introduction

In a psychology class I was taking a few years ago, there was a debate about a video we had watched on the Milgram experiment on obedience to authority figures, which was a series of social psychology experiments conducted by Yale University psychologist Stanley Milgram. These experiments measured the willingness of study participants, men from a diverse range of occupations with varying levels of education, to obey an authority figure who instructed them to perform acts conflicting with their personal conscience; the experiment found, unexpectedly, that a very high proportion of people were prepared to obey, albeit unwillingly, even if apparently causing serious injury and distress.

I had never seen the video before and could not believe that people would continue to give another person (who also had a heart condition) an electric shock that could potentially kill him. I remember listening to my classmates saying how under pressure they could see how it was possible to just continue giving shocks. To me I just couldn't accept what they were saying.

I said, "What about personal responsibility? You have a choice. You don't have to follow what anyone else is saying."

The debate continued, but I could not change how I

felt – that I wouldn't have cared what the authority figure was telling me, I would have made my own decision. That principle has stuck with me my whole life. I have sought to discover and understand for myself who I am, why I exist, and the reason I am in a physical life. I have not looked outside myself for answers but within.

My journey of discovery within started a long time ago when I first challenged the idea of God or the divine intelligence. I was at a Christmas service, singing the praises of God in a hymn, and all of a sudden I thought, Why I am singing these words? I don't believe in a God that has been taught to me by other people. I'm not singing something I don't believe in! That thought didn't go away, and in the evening as I lay in bed thinking about it, I asked, if there really was a God or spirit or something listening, for that thing to answer me and let me know.

A few moments later I heard a man's voice inside my head say, "I am here."

Startled and a bit in shock, I kept listening to see if I could hear anything else. After a while I had convinced myself that I must have made it all up, that it was just my imagination.

The next moment I heard the same man's voice say, "It wouldn't matter what we said to you; it would never be enough proof!"

From that moment on my life changed. I started on a journey of understanding that life is more than just the physical presence we know. I have been a student, open to receive knowledge of my existence, my understanding of God, the divine intelligence, the oneness, or any other name you wish to call the divine presence that is a part of us all that is always reaching out to us to wake up and realise how much more there is to learn and understand.

I was given the words below as a guide to understanding how living, dying, and eternity are all a cycle that is endless, limitless, and open for us all to access the moment we decide to, and maybe the reason you are reading these words now.

Maybe you are also starting to feel that something just isn't right, that there has to be more than just this life, and the moment you ask the question *who am I?* the floodgates of learning open up if you are willing and courageous enough to explore the full potential of who you are and the endless, limitless potential of your soul, energy, or life force that can be miraculous if you choose to let the divine oneness flow through you.

Physical Existence Is a Hologram for Spiritual Practise

You do not come to this world by chance. You choose this lifetime, this experience, to know yourself. When you have decided who you are and what you are being, you then decide to go experience this until you decide it no longer fits your understanding. And so you go back and evaluate your life again until you decide who you next want to be and how you are being—this goes on indefinitely. You choose the circumstance of your life, and the rest is free will for you to interpret as you go along your pathway.

The meaning of all things is to discover who you are

and what you are being until it no longer suits you, until eventually you discover that there has to be more than the accumulation of physical objects. No shiny bauble will ever be enough to fill the void, and one day, you realise the creative force is calling you – not in the physical element but in the spiritual element. You feel it burning in you like a fire that will not be put out, until everything feels wrong and out of place and you need to discover what this unknown, unseen longing is.

When you reach that point, you can only go within and sit with the power of spiritual connection, for there you will find answers to your questions. Then and only then can you set forth the practise of this knowledge through your experiences. So it is a chain reaction of living, experiencing, gaining knowledge, going within, being reborn into living, gaining experiences, and seeking more knowledge, until at last the understanding of who you are and what you are being becomes clear. You realise you are one with the creative force made manifest, that the physical existence is a hologram for spiritual practise— to learn and gain understanding. Then you can say, "I will choose another experience," and you may then seek experiences in altering realities.

Yes, this is possible and not as far-fetched as you might think. My guides have always taught me that if something offends my logic, not to dismiss it out of hand, but to file it away for another day, as it takes time to absorb and digest new ideas and make sense of them. As you progress in your understanding, the once-new ideas that have been filed away then feel more of a logical next step. With that in mind, I hope you too are inspired to ask, *Who am I?* as we share the journey together as both student and teacher, exploring the next step of our evolution, the blooming into consciousness of our spiritual selves whilst here in the physical.

Chapter 1

YOUR PHYSICAL LIFE IS AN ILLUSION

With love in our hearts we walk with you
blooming into consciousness as one.

[I have included in this chapter questions I have asked my guide about how we are consciously evolving in the physical and their answers in response.]

The mind in all its glory feels the need to embrace change, but the soul needs nothing. It needs nothing to fulfil itself for its purpose is to "be"; therefore, it is already "being" now. What form it takes is quite another matter. Your existence here upon the earth plane is transitory. Your soul is capable of being everywhere at once, for it is the oneness being, a part of which is here in the physical realm. We have broken our own consciousness into infinitesimal pieces and scattered them to the wind.

The experiences of each one of us, therefore, are the unique separate pieces of soul individuated into the physical made manifest. Now the soul is the one whole piece that is like a magnet drawing the separate piece back. So you are journeying back to soul, but you are doing or being it via the physical. So you are trying to connect physical attributes, the physical body, to the consciousness. It is akin to a slice of pear being pushed through a sieve to reconnect back to a whole pear. It cannot work. So how did you individuate into a single unique piece of soul in the physical? The answer is you did not. You did not separate at all. You have built an illusionary world so that you may know yourself. The soul or oneness is completely intact and connected to all, all at once, all of the time. So what you are effectively doing is using the conscious mind to undergo a series of experiences to reconnect to the unconscious (in the physical) mind.

You have not been far away from the understanding. All you needed to do was open the curtains or the window to the realty that you are but a reflection of a piece of the oneness knowing thyself.

{That doesn't make sense to me?}

All things become clear when you stop stirring the mud. In other words, calm your mind, the waters settle, and you see a mirror image. The reflection in the water isn't the real you. Although your presence and reflection is on the surface of the water, it is just that, a reflection.

{Yes, but the reflection can't move without the person moving, so how can we be physically moving?}

The principle is the same. You are the reflection animated by the soul enlivened by the original you.

You are source energy first; this, we have agreed. Now you think you are separate from source in the physical as you incarnate and your vibration is slower and the illusion of time gives you the illusion of separateness, but you are never separate from source. Always, the whole remains as consciousness.

You are but a mere infinitesimal piece of you in the physical, being enlivened by the source which is also you residing in the divine intelligence, consciousness or God. In other words, you are in both spirit and physical at the same time. You are just unaware of the spiritual you until you learn to access that part of you that resides in the divine consciousness.

To do this, your most important task is to quiet the mind and go within in stillness and meditation.

Imagine it like this: Think of a volcano that has poured lava down a hillside. As it cools, so the lava changes form into a rock. It is still part of the volcano, only it does not know it is lava anymore. If you were to return the rock to the source or volcano, it would quickly revert back to lava once more and be as one. You are the rock that does not know it is one with its source until it returns.

You Are as a Rose Blooming into the Physical

{Why do we feel like we are in control or feel we are the one who is in control?}

My child that is a good question. It comes back to consciousness.

You are in control, but you will only recognise this if your awareness of you as source is raised. You are unable to recognise it if you are being a rock.

To raise your vibration and forgive us for repeating ourselves, your most important task is to quiet the mind and go within in stillness and meditation.

If you choose to be conscious, you can reflect your energy into anything, anywhere, anytime. Therefore, your gods are not your gods but your own consciousness made manifest.

{Ok. So God is me. I am God everywhere and all the time. What on earth am I doing giving myself such a hard time. What's the point of hiding myself or bits of my own self or conscious awareness – to what end?}

My child you are divinity in expression. You are constantly changing form through expression. The oneness is everything, everywhere; you are creating a new form within the oneness.

{I'm still not clear? If divinity is perfect, what's the point, there is no evolution!}

My child, evolution is consciousness, oneness. It is knowing thyself.

{That's still not enough for me to make sense of it?}

A rose is already a rose, is it not?

{Yes.}

But the rose can change form. It can create or be new colours, new without thorns, multicoloured, scented, not scented. All these can be the rose, which is already perfect. It needs no thing to be a rose, but experiences give it more awareness of itself and the ability to be more in different ways. That is like you as a sentient being in the physical; you are expressing different ways of knowing thyself.

Chapter 2

TO BLOOM OR NOT TO BLOOM

And the day came when the risk to remain
tight in a bud was more painful than the
risk it took to blossom.

– Anaïs Nin

A Change of Attitude

During the war, a woman went to live with her husband
in a camp on the Mojave Desert. She simply hated the
place; the heat was almost unbearable: 125 degrees in the
shade, wind blowing incessantly, and there was sand –
sand everywhere. Finally, in desperation she wrote to her
parents in Ohio and said that she couldn't stand it another
minute and was coming home.

Very quickly came the reply by airmail from her
father – just the two familiar lines: "Two men looked
out from prison bars. One saw the mud; the other saw
stars." The daughter did some real thinking, not just
intellectually, but with her heart also. She decided to stay
at her post. She made friends with the natives, learned to
love the country, and eventually wrote a book about it. The

desert hadn't changed, but her attitude had, and because she listened with her heart to the words her father sent, a whole *new world* opened up to her. (Unknown author)

If we are looking out of the prison bars, some of us see mud, which we could term the *physical reality*, and some of us see stars, which could be termed as the *spiritual self, higher self, divine consciousness* or *God*, and think that they are separate. Very few of us combine the two and are aware that we coexist in the physical with the divine consciousness or God simultaneously. If we change our attitude as the daughter did and look with our intellect and our hearts and see the two as one as they coexist, a whole *new world* opens up to us.

Chapter 3

LIVING A LOW-LEVEL EXISTENCE

If you are going to work only to pay the bills and you slump back home tired, unhappy, and depleted of energy only to do the same thing tomorrow, then you are living a low-level existence.

I wonder how many cave people committed suicide? Did they throw in the towel one day and say, "It's too difficult to hunt, the mammoths see me a mile away, and I can't keep up with them, so I'm going to throw myself under their feet instead!" I suspect that no matter how difficult it got, cave people never gave up, because their survival depended on it. More importantly, they had the means within themselves to take control of the situation. If they were hungry, they went out and hunted or collected fruits and berries or other natural food. They were empowered, because they had a choice to react however they wanted as it was within their means.

Many people that would be classed as uncivilised in today's society live in tribes that have that same system in place of empowerment and sense of family and community. It may be a difficult life at times for them as they face the natural elements and it's probably something that we wouldn't want to go back to, but to move forward or evolve as a human species that thrives, taking the best of those situations and bringing them into your life, will help change your own personal life from low-level existing to high-level thriving!

If you equate that to today's way of living, we choose jobs that may start out as OK, but as we move forward, we can feel trapped, as we are not able to just go out and get food if we haven't got enough money. We haven't got land to feed us, and where families previously had to stick together for survival, we now separate more easily, thinking we have an independent income and can manage and become isolated or struggle to survive and get help from the government. We may not all have families that support us, but we can choose the people we hang out with. We can choose to have them in our lives, supporting each other as we navigate through difficult times, and there is never a more difficult time for us than the time of change.

There are a lot of people consciously waking up on the planet today. By that I mean we are evolving as a species consciously. We are realising that there has to be a better way of life than living to pay the bills! It is an existence that feels limiting and fear based. If we move out of our comfort zones and embrace new ideas about ourselves, then we fear not being able to pay the bills, not being able to pay for a roof over our heads, and we slink back into the low-level existing again. It's a pattern that repeats over and over again until we reach a breaking point. Some people come to me after feeling that they have lost everything – their financial security, their family ties, and their senses of direction and purpose. They are dejected and depressed and feel like giving up. The first thing I say to them is the hardest part is over, and you are still here, living, breathing, and functioning.

When I say high-level thriving, I mean understanding who we really are. We are a spiritual essence or divine energy or intelligence that is housed in a physical body. If you have found this book and read through to this chapter, then you are realising that you had choices before you came, and you have choices now.

Chapter 4

CHANGE

In this moment of now, your evolution has been very much based on the physical environment that you are accustomed to living in. Were you to say, for example (like your Tardis), stay completely encapsulated in it, you would still search within. Now if you are powerful enough, you would eventually connect to divine consciousness and eventually transmute your body into the divine consciousness (yes, it can be done). Miracles we seek are not miracles but potentially unexplored abilities yet to be attuned to the vibrational match of divine consciousness, intelligence, or God, all of which are the same term for unconditional love. If you are in the box and not developed enough you could go mad and lose your mind to the ego, for the ego will seek refuge without – meaning it will look for outside sources and influences to determine who you are at this time.

We are all in the physical working alongside other people. Even if we are only visiting the supermarket once a week and only seeing the people there and maybe not even speaking, we have joined other energies. It is enough to remind you of the world and the place you take in the world. When you are being spiritual, you walk alone for a while as you sort out the definition of who you are and who you are becoming.

Tuning In to Your Frequency

As you raise your vibration and attune to the higher frequencies, you start to become out of vibrational alignments with yourself as well as others as you try to match up your vibration to source. It is like trying to tune in to a radio station on a different frequency than the one you are currently on; there is an adjusting into the frequency before you can hear the signal clearly. As you start to adjust into these higher vibrations or frequencies, you may start encountering difficulties in your life. It might be in a relationship, it may be at work, or it may even be with yourself, and no matter where you are, you may start feeling unhappy or unsettled.

Change happens and we can either direct it by deciding what's right for us, or we can allow change to happen, dictated by other people's choices as a result of our non-action. For example, say you saw a beautiful house and wanted to buy it, as it seemed perfect, but you were undecided and you couldn't make up your mind what to do. Then as you were deciding, someone else comes along and buys it. You may feel disappointment, but the person who bought the house was tuned into their frequency, and it was a natural flow. You had not been able to decide as you were wavering in frequency (between stations), so those who were more aligned made the decision for you.

It's OK and perfectly normal to have these moments of struggle, as indecision often happens when we are moving forward into change. Sometimes we fight it because the familiar, even if it is not great and is making us unhappy, is better than the fear of the unknown. Yet it is my experience that the very change we fear is often our biggest road to freedom. When it feels like everything is falling apart in your life, this deconstruction is exactly what your soul has asked for.

You may not recognise change as a means to an end, but even when you fear change and see it as just another hurdle or obstacle that is making your life miserable, it can actually be the opposite; it can actually lead to your greatest source of happiness.

Fearing Change

There is nothing more life deadening than being stagnant, fearing change, and closing down to life. We become protective and try to hang on to the familiar, and it results in pain for us and others involved when we fight the inevitable. Even if we feel we have thwarted change and managed to create a holding place where we hold the status quo, it is a place of fear, waiting constantly for the walls of our glass palace to crash, as we cannot fight the universal force of our own soul which has been asking for change.

The universal force or soul does not know fear, ego, or any other human emotion or barrier that we create. We are all born of the one source, and we incarnate into this life with an emerging identity that we are collecting as a database of experiences, and changes are necessary as we raise our vibration. It may feel like a tremendous uphill struggle to incorporate change when we are out of sync with others around us, even loved ones. We feel unfulfilled, confused, and unsure of what is going on. Our egos may tell us we are even going mad, but we tell you: you are not!

You are feeling the evolutionary pull that will jump evolution into the next phase. Now, here is the most important thing you will ever read: if you do not consciously make the jump, you will fall into oblivion, left behind as a casualty of the war of the ego. For to not take the next step, to not consciously evolve, is to choose to stay behind, left in the physical environment that serves the universe as a ground for new energies that are evolving. If you do not raise your game, so to speak, you will be the Neanderthal that is stuck in the physical, unable to retain consciousness, for the consciousness of the evolved – the ones who wake up, who choose consciously to believe and move forward, knowing that consciousness is the new awareness needed to divine understanding – will leave, and you will not have the energy on the physical plane for your own evolution once you are left behind.

Parental Figure of Humanity

The energy left once consciousness moves forward will have a new beginning, but at the beginning. You will not consciously know yourselves as you do now, and you will inherit the legacy of the ego.

If you can, on the other hand, choose to consciously start delving into this new understanding, you start becoming attuned to a higher frequency which then joins with others on that frequency and then makes the whole, and the whole can then move forward. Now the question you may be asking at this time is: How will I know if I am aware? Then the thought you may be thinking is, This all sounds absurd!

The first thought shows your consciousness is already being raised; the second is your ego blocking your path. If you give in to the ego, you will be the cave person of the past. If you go with, OK, help me out here, how can I start to understand, then you are on the jump pathway. We can tell you scientists have known for a long while about the ability to jump frequencies that move matter into another realm. What they do not understand is that science alone cannot solve evolution. It is not a problem but a solution to understand who you are.

When you recognise you are the divine incarnate, you open the possibility of the miracle, which is your highly evolved and attuned understanding. Without divine intention, you cannot move the evolution of the human species forward. Scientists learn to jump forward without a parachute into the abyss of the ego. It is akin to a baby crawling along a mountain ledge unattended. Eventually the baby is going to fall off without guidance from a higher awareness, such as a parent who has more knowledge of his or her abilities as a baby and the environment they are in. The divine consciousness, oneness, source, intelligence, or God, is, for want of another word, the parental figure to humanity, guiding us not to fall off the ledge. Science without the presence of the unconditional love of divine consciousness is the unattended baby on the mountain ledge.

The Jump Pathway

And now something that is going to change the way many think: you can be eternal in the physical when you have learned to jump into the higher dimensions through raised consciousness. Wow! Mind-blowing! So, you see, science is a powerful ally into the evolutionary jump, but it will not be able to do it alone. It will help the people who need structured analysis of the science to gain belief, but it will not suffice alone. We can tell you the misery of the ones left behind will be felt by the consciousness. It is the conscious who send the higher energies from the higher dimensions into the physical. This constant bombardment of physical and conscious energy gives you access, gives you a chance to join them. We wish no soul to be left behind, but you have free will, and you have a choice, but always we will be by your side until you better understand the glorious future that awaits you and humanity at this juncture in the physical environment.

Allowing Change

Asking yourself these questions will help you to recognise where you are in your life right now and what may be holding you back through fear--based thoughts. Be as honest as you can.

- In this moment of now, what is important to me?
- In my life now, what do I think is holding me back?

- What am I prepared to let go of that doesn't feel right any longer?

Accept and make peace with your life no matter what is going on and ask yourself now: what is the one change that I can make in my life, no matter how small, that will make me feel better or happier?

Remember: your soul knows exactly how you feel and will only respond to what is in your heart calling it to you, whether it is fear based or positive and loving.

Chapter 5

WAKING UP!

There is a start and an end to all things. If you believe that life continues after you pass off the physical body and into the realm of spirit or heaven or divine consciousness, then you shall be awake quickly, for you are already partially awake once you acknowledge that death is not possible. The soul cannot die; however, it can change form. As ice melts, so the soul reverts back to its original state; the soul can be more than the "totality of now" that you are experiencing. It can be the whole of everything once it becomes known to itself. In other words, when you become aware that you are a mere reflection, a portion of the whole reflected to the experience of now, when you understand this, then you can begin to know yourself.

Imagine you, or your unique personality, is just like a drop of water from the ocean that has splashed onto a bird's wing and dropped onto a mountain ledge. You, the drop which contains everything known from the whole sea is now contained within the droplet, but once you move away from the sea, you lose consciousness of the whole that you are a part of. You are now experiencing the moment on the mountain ledge as a unique, individual piece of the whole as though you are alone. You have forgotten where you came from, but the whole sea is still within you and has not forgotten. When you feel the whole stirring within you as it calls you to remember who you are, you may become agitated or restless as though trying to fit something together but you are not quite sure what.

You may have everything you could ever want in life, a fantastic relationship, family, friends, successful career, and great health, but it still doesn't feel enough. That restlessness is the larger part within you, the soul that has no time that is always in the present which is asking you to re-remember or wake up into the consciousness of the whole whilst you are still experiencing your mountain ledge or living in the physical.

It is your birthright to have access to the whole oneness within where all is possible, so anything you can think of or imagine, you have access to, absolutely anything, whether it is talking to your loved ones who have passed who are also a part of the whole sea or your existence in altering realities, such as your unique droplet separating and dropping on to two separate mountain ledges. Both forget where they came from, both think they are alone, yet both contain the whole within them but exist in alternate realities as well as existing in the reality of the oneness. In other words, when you become aware that you are a mere reflection, a portion of the whole reflected to the experience of now, you would remember you were part of the whole sea and call forth its properties within you. The power of the oneness or the whole sea then flows through you.

When you understand this, then you can begin to know yourself.

On the Mountain Ledge of Physical Existence

As the droplet, you are now on the mountain ledge of physical existence. You are experiencing the separation or feeling of aloneness. You have also forgotten the whole sea or soul which you are a part of, and you are experiencing your life as a unique individual whose concept of self is one of separation or existence other than part of the whole oneness or sea that you came from.

Your experiences are now shaping your existence and perception of who you are. You are, however, also existing in a multidimensionality reality. You are the droplet on the physical mountain ledge, but you are also part of every other single droplet that has also landed on the mountain ledge from the whole sea or oneness or soul, each having landed on the mountain ledge and forgotten the sea from whence they came and are formed from.

When we die or go back to the sea, the soul or the oneness, we retain our unique identities or personalities that we know as ourselves, but we are also one with the whole oneness which exists eternally, so our existing is happening all at once in the sea or soul or oneness in the "no time", whilst also being a part of the other droplets who have also separated on the mountain ledge and are still residing in the physical. In the physical, as we forget the whole sea or soul, we forget we are one. We forget everything other than our experience of the physical environment we are in. Our only focus is the physical.

We focus on our everyday lives as though that is our only existence and reality. As we keep forgetting the whole sea or soul that we came from which is a divine vibration of unconditional love so our vibration lowers, it becomes slower and denser, and the more we forget, the more we move away from our inheritance of power. We then seek power in the physical as separate, unconnected beings. So now we have isolated ourselves from the oneness, and as a single, separate physical being on the earth, our physical form goes on a journey to gain experiences to help us re-remember who we are as we seek to reconnect back to our true source or home.

> Don't you know yet?
> It is your light that lights the worlds.
>
> —Rumi

Chapter 6

IS THE SPIRIT WORLD REAL?

How do you explain 3D from a 1D standpoint? How do you explain the colour blue to a person who has been blind from birth? At this time, we have limited capabilities with which to grasp what the spirit world – or heaven, as some would call it – is like. We are trying to understand the meaning of a limitless, infinite, immortal intelligence way beyond our comprehension of it here. Can you teach a newborn baby how to fly an aeroplane? No. Neither can you explain the world the baby is growing up in until its mind is mature enough and has grown enough to comprehend what you are describing. So we filter our understanding through what we observe here until it no longer serves us to do so.

We go through those experiences of bad things happening and awaken ourselves, and our minds open enough to start grasping the new concepts about who we are and where we are going back to after we die.

In the illusion of physical life we are living, there is nothing separate from the whole sea or oneness. Our physical mountain ledge is still part of the whole. It is created by the whole sea or oneness and vibrates at a different pace or speed which gives us the illusion of physical reality and our feeling of separateness. We each are vibrating at different speeds, or, less or more connectedness to the whole oneness. And depending on the rate of our vibration, we are attracting to us people who are on the same vibration as ourselves, and this changes according to our response to situations in our lives. It is only when we reach a level of inner calm from those ongoing experiences that we start to glimpse the world of spirit or the sea or oneness that we go home to. So in effect, the spirit world is as real to you as the level of consciousness that you have attained whilst here in the physical.

Those more highly attuned to the divine frequencies share their understanding, but it is only from their viewpoint. Each person will have a unique perspective of the spirit world depending on his or her experiences that are filtered through their physical brains. That is where the confusion becomes apparent, for you have to go within and connect to source to attain a picture closest to your vibration in spirit.

Our vibration is how we hold our places in the spiritual realm. We are resonating at a certain frequency of consciousness, and we are vibrating there with others who are on the same level. The light can move down to a certain degree to lesser vibrating souls, but the lesser cannot move higher into the light unless they become in tune with that vibrational energy, which happens through those experience that we keep perpetuating in the physical and other dimensions.

Your higher self, or the part of you that is consciousness residing in spirit and a part of the whole oneness, is like a library where you can go and look up and read your past experiences or remember them. It feels like a déjà vu experience where you reconnect to your higher self – you suddenly know. You remember being in a particular place or you know or remember someone you just don't know how you know. That is you accessing your higher self and all your experiences, or rejoining the oneness.

We often choose to come back to the physical earth plane with the same people and re-enact the same experiences if we did not fully realise what we wanted to achieve in the experience the first time around. So then we form bonds with other people or soul groups and soulmates. Soulmates are the people whom you feel an instant connection with. Even if they are total strangers, you still feel that connection or matching vibrational wave you both are vibrating on. They are often our greatest teachers.

Although there is no time in spirit, we have time in the physical as our vibration is much slower than when we are in spirit, which then gives us the illusion of time here. In the slowed vibration of the physical, past lives to us feel real, but it is not past. Every single incarnation whilst in a time sense is trillions or countless. All of those are happening in this very moment. Stretch that very moment out as a slowed vibration, and we create past and future and the illusion of time. That is how we describe reincarnation or past lives, they are not past lives so much as our slowed vibration, the moment you refocus or rejoin the oneness, or return home to spirit, you have access to everything at once in the multidimensional universe, but in the physical we have forgotten this understanding, and we are caught in the illusion of time.

To explain this further, look at the body you are in. Look at the shape of your hands. Look in the mirror at the colour of your eyes. Run your fingers down your cheeks and jawbone and feel the contours of your face. You chose the body you are in before you came into the physical. You knew the genes of your parents and the colour that your hair, eyes, and skin would be. You knew how tall or short you would be. You knew you would be disabled or whether you had chosen to have the body fit for an athlete. You chose the beautiful voice, the acting ability, or the ability to be bilingual – all of those decisions were made or chosen by you before you came.

What you left to be decided was your reaction to those choices and how you were to use those inherent abilities that you came here with.

Have you ever heard someone sing or play an instrument and wonder why they were not making a living at it, as they were so good? They will have garnered that ability over many lifetimes in the physical, but in the lifetime they are having now, they may want to work on something else. They may want to learn to write or be a scientist or a chef or just a mother or father or family member for their own personal reasons of growth.

They may even have chosen the experience of being homeless before they incarnated into the physical, as they knew it will push them to answer the call of divinity or ask much bigger questions as to the meaning of their existences.

If you have ever been in a state of desperate unhappiness

and come out the other side wiser and stronger for the experience, or maybe someone else you know has, your strength to overcome those obstacles is what inspires others to keep going and reach for their full potentials too.

When you stop sweating the small stuff, a whole new world opens up. You become freer in your "beingness" and start making decisions based on what you feel within from that new don't-sweat-the-small-stuff perspective. You start to make choices on what feels good rather than what is expected of you and find yourself feeling empowered by the inspiration that follows.

When you then follow that inspiration and start doing things that make your feel alive, you feel more connected to the whole or the greater part of you, both here and in the realm of infinite intelligence, God, or divine oneness that is you at its best.

Successful people live their dreams through inspiration, the feeling of being at one with that inspiration, be it painting, teaching, or just doing something for the sheer fun of it.

Success is subjective in the eyes of each of us. For some, success is defined by the accumulation of wealth. Perhaps it would be a better definition to say that success is the result of being inspired into feeling at one with your true self and following that passion. At each step of following your heart, you are being successful, and the end product is a reflection of your inspired action. Remember: you are a mere reflection of the oneness, a droplet of life projected into the physical. You have all the elements of the power of creation within you as part of the ultimate omnipotence of infinite intelligence. You, as part of that infinite intelligence, once you wake up and realise this, can then reflect anything you desire into your perceived reality of now.

If you are not able to grasp that fully yet, following your heart is the next best thing, for that feeling of desire is your manifesting ability.

The only way we can make sense of it here is to break it down. We come to the physical with other people or souls who are on our vibrational level and part of our soul groups. We have agreed the circumstance and the major life events – such as major illnesses, accidents, and deaths (even our own) – that we are going to be a part of. We choose each other. You choose the mother or father that you love or hate. The absent parent, the violent sibling, the loving and kind family member and friends good and bad are all agreed. We then add to that our free will or how we respond to the challenges that have come our way.

Our free will dictates the path we take and the experience we are gaining as a result of the circumstances we are undergoing. It is when we are under extreme stress that we often turn to God or spirit for help or answers, and it doesn't matter what term you use for the divine source; it serves as an opening for the same family and friends that you agreed would stay behind in spirit to help you out and watch over you. These are your guides, family members, and angels who will all be part of your soul group on the same vibrational level as you.

From the spiritual realm you see your loved ones as energy or like a glowing light of pure energy. Remember: you do not need any physical body in spirit, so we see the pure energy of our loved ones on the earth plane in their true form as glowing energy too, which makes perfect sense as we feel the connection though our linked energy which is part of the whole oneness. In that energy connection we can communicate telepathically or via the senses of clairaudience, clairvoyance, clairsentience, and more.

- Clairaudience (clear hearing, or psychic hearing)
- Clairvoyance (clear seeing, or psychic vision)
- Clairsentience (clear sensing or psychic feeling/ sensing, including clairempathy)

Holding Spiritual Focus

There is an expansive version of ourselves in spirit that sees everything in real time, or no time, meaning we see all of our lives being played out in the multidimensional universes whilst also being aware we are in the physical as well. It is just that part of the energy of you that agreed to others holding spiritual focus so they could give direct help to loved ones and you in the physical.

You may be doing exactly the same for them in another time-space reality where you are holding the focus of staying in spirit to help them in the dimension they are in; you just don't know you are doing it because your focus at this present time is only a fraction of who you are, and is specifically focused to just be aware of the physical. Sorry if that's long-winded, but again it's down to interpretation of a complex understanding.

If you think about the you in spirit now, you are not in a physical body nor restricted to time, as everything is happening at once, you can realise that you can put your focus on to any part of you at any time in your lives in the physical realm or other dimensions and be aware of all of them. You then are doing this collectively with your soul group as a whole. So you can be aware of the past, present, and future of physical existence, put your focus on any particular time, and be totally aware of your needs at any time. If you can think of something in the spirit world, you can create it instantaneously, you can even slow down the vibration a little to feel more of the experience similar to the physical experience. You, as an energy form, can be anywhere. You can fly, listen to every conversation you ever had all at once, and now you see the depth of the experience you can have in spiritual terms.

When people ask me, "Has my loved one who passed before me moved on and forgotten me?" I always say they can never forget, and as there is no time, they will be able to be with you every moment of every second and are never really apart from you, and although they can be anywhere in an alternate universe, they can be in both places at once. In fact, they can be everywhere at once, so they are never held back or waiting. They are always present with you by their ability to have a much bigger, expanded ability to focus everywhere at once yet still be right by your side.

Just to add to the complexity of this, as you are part of the oneness and only a fraction of you is reflected into this physical illusion or hologram of earthy life, you are in fact never, ever separate from the one you love, for they too, in effect, are a mere fraction of themselves focused into the physical realm, and the larger expanded version of themselves is residing in spirit with you as part of the whole consciousness – just saying!

In regard to the light levels in spirit, there are degrees of light that we each attain and move forward into. There is also more than the oneness, if you can comprehend that! Something more, even brighter than the whole oneness yet for us to discover!

Chapter 7

MEDITATION AND WHY IT WORKS

We are vibrational beings having a physical experience. We have said this often. So now to experience your soul or the spiritual part of you, you have to imagine what it would be like to have all that energy with no physical body to exert itself through. You would be left with pure, positive, unconditional love, able to be in multidimensional universes!

Put the shell of the physical body back around the pure, positive energy, and it is like wrapping a blanket around a speaker to muffle the noise. The communication is not clear, and the reason you are at the next chapter in human life in the physical, the ability to reconnect with the true source of who you are.

So we have source energy, and we have the body, a finely tuned mechanism with everything that you need to recognise the true source of yourself.

Apart from time in the physical, you have no restrictions. Time is the critical factor in understanding how we can connect. When you are attuning to spirit and working with spirit, everything vibrates at a very high speed until eventually it seems to slow down and stop. That is the connection with the no time, or oneness.

It is a bit contradictory to say you have to speed up your vibration to reach a slower vibration, but that is not exactly accurate. It is not a slower vibration, although it seems that way, but a perfect vibration of no time.

To do that in the physical is something we are working towards – purity of thoughts in allowing the flow of unconditional love.

To tune in we are each having our own experience, but the more we stay in the high-energy frequencies, the more aligned we become.

Tuning into Your Inner Guidance and Intuition

Meditation comes in many forms. You can be detached enough from reality to go into spirit and communicate with your guides, angels, and loved ones, and you can also look along the timeline and see past and future events.

There is also the kind of meditation that you can do just listening to relaxing music, which switches off the chatter of the mind, and then there is the waking mediation that you can do in communication as in mediumship and channelling. This is just ordinary breathing in and out in a peaceful way.

Any form of relaxing the mind and letting go benefits your whole well-being. When you meditate and move your focus out of the daily vibrational energy and focus into a calm and peaceful state, you start to connect with the divine flow. You move into an allowing state, which is when you drop the barriers or thought trails (your intentions and connectedness with divine consciousness) that you have been using to block the flow of divinity to you.

We have spoken about meditation and connecting with your guides, and this has a knock on effect in your daily lives. Being at one, being at peace, and taking time every day to connect contributes to your thoughts you are sending out.

To connect with divinity is to connect the energy that creates your reality, and this continues through each lifetime, and when you go back home to spirit, you see from your free will what you have created and what you wish to work on next time. These moments build into each incarnation.

You do not hold any karma that people speak of, as we have said that everything you do is a choice.

When you come back to work on something, the experience you are going through has been chosen by you, but as you start to awaken from your spiritual slumber, you realise creating positive thoughts has a positive momentum that keeps going.

You have built up many, many lifetimes of thoughts that you have desired or not desired, and some have played out and some not. With each incarnation you start to get a glimpse of your pathway and the road to understanding, which is to align your thoughts into spiritual awareness, for when you build your conscious awareness and others also do the same, you raise your vibration to a higher level.

We talk all the time of spiritual vibration, but it takes no action to align. We spend many different ways struggling with actions that do not feel right in our hearts instead of listening to our path that feels good to walk, and so the resistance keeps building, and we look for experiences to snap us out of it.

When you start to meditate each day, even for a few minutes, you start to build a new thought trail, one that is directly connected to spirit and divine intention or unconditional love without interruption of the lower physical vibrations.

In that place of pure connection and unconditional love, all problems are shown for what they are, created by you and through your focus in the illusion of the physical. We say illusion, as you are nothing but a reflection of spirit creating at will. When you grasp that concept, you then have to let the current thought trails drop back and go into mediation which then connects to pure positive energy of divinity which is you and flowing through you.

Meditation Serves Several Purposes

1. To put your physical life back into balance by stopping the stressed or negative thought patterns reoccurring by breaking them with the peaceful energy that connects back to your true self
2. To strengthen your connection to your true spiritual nature
3. To allow your guides and angels to start working with you, developing your energy fields to become more receptive to spirit, which starts to give you a heightened awareness of who you are being
4. To change the way you view situations

The ultimate purpose of meditation is to take you back home into spirit, to connect and allow the flow of your true source to filter into your daily life, whether it is to stop and become realigned in vibration or to increase your capacity to connect with spirit or to be aware how your intention to focus becomes more attuned after you have reconnected with source.

These are all reasons that you may start seeing the beneficial effects of meditation, which is really alignment back to the unconditional flow of love that is you in your truest form.

The more you connect to the source within, the higher your raise your vibration and the easier it becomes to bring that into your daily lives. Every time you meditate your whole body, every single cell aligns into well-being as you let the source flow through you.

It is only your limited beliefs that disconnect from that well-being, and you create ailments once more.

It sounds easy to say, but at least understanding how you can heal though meditation or the flow of source can give comfort in the knowledge that we may not be capable yet of believing in the power of the divine source, but it can create what we would call "miracles of healing", which is nothing more than your perfect alignment with wellness.

Anything you want to achieve has its answer in mediation, for you then line up with the divine flow, which is perfect, and if you allow the flow to be at one with you and let it flow through you, your whole physical body and mental thoughts will start to project that well-being.

Complete This Exercise

Breathing into Peace Meditation

- Create a space somewhere that you can relax in. It might be the corner of a room or a whole room, but make sure you will be able to spend time there undisturbed.
- Start by clearing away any clutter so that it feels relaxing.
- Next, make this space your own. You can keep it minimalist, or you can put plants, crystals, pictures, ornaments, or anything that makes you feel calm and peaceful around you.
- Use candles to create soft lighting, and if you want an aroma to fill the air, use incense sticks or use a diffuser with essential oils or anything that you wish.
- If you want to play music or listen to a guided mediation, make sure you have a device that's easy to use in your space.
- Once you have created your space, set a time each day that you will be able to spend in meditation undisturbed.
- Now you have your set space and time, sit quietly. Light your candles and use your aroma and music to soothe and relax you, or just sit quietly without them if you prefer.
- I want you to close your eyes and focus on your breathing. Breathe in deeply through your nose and out through your mouth three times.

- Keep focusing on your breathing, and as you inhale, say in your mind, "This is my time. I allow myself to relax."
- Keep your focus on breathing deeply two more times and say, "I am powerful. I am at peace."
- Send your thoughts of love and appreciation for the present moment and, breathing deeply once more, allow yourself to come back to the room and open your eyes.

This exercise is a practise to get you comfortable with your surroundings and into the habit of relaxing every time you are in your own quiet mediation space.

Practise every day for at least five to ten minutes just to get you into the peaceful energy needed for mediation.

As you read through the book, you will get to chapters that have deeper mediation exercises and guided meditations. If you are meditating alone, it may take you a while to learn the steps of the meditation. To help you remember the steps, you can also ask someone you feel comfortable meditating with to read the steps aloud for you.

If you have been creating a peaceful, relaxed state doing this exercise every day, then the other mediation techniques will be easier for you to achieve as you are further along into the relaxed state of mind needed to connect deeper into the divine consciousness or oneness.

Chapter 8

WHY DO BAD THINGS KEEP HAPPENING TO ME?

There are many masters disguised as the most vulnerable of us on the planet today.

As a psychic medium, counsellor, and life coach, I come across various types of people in life. I see people from differing countries and religions with problems that are personal to them and their families. The most important thing I have learned in my work is that no matter what country you are from, what religion you believe in, what sexuality you are, we are all individually trying to understand our own personal world. Some are surviving. Others are stuck in grief and unhappiness, and some are making their ways forward in careers, relationships, and life.

No matter what stage you are at in life, there are times when we become out of alignment with source and our world feels like it is falling apart. We are unable to see our way forward. These are the times that we are starting our own personal journeys of enlightenment. We are embarking on the journey we agreed before we came here. Whether you believe in the afterlife or not, you are still living, breathing, and going through the same life as everyone else on the planet – your personal journey. And this journey starts way before you were born to the earth; it starts in spirit. You agree to your family, your friends, everyone who has an impact on your life. You decide what experiences you wish to feel and live in physically, and then you agree to people that will come along to help you.

Now here is where it gets a bit tricky, so bear with me. You choose the people that give you the best and the worst experiences. (You may have to allow that to settle for a while). The first thing I hear you say is, "But I would not choose to have any harm come to my family or watch a loved one suffer an illness." But it isn't as simple as that. Each one of us is choosing an experience. We are then choosing others to help us experience it. Let us first delve into spiritual understanding here for a moment. When you die or pass over into the spiritual realm, you are not your physical body any more. You are part of the one soul again. You retain your identity, the uniqueness of you, your spiritual blueprint of all your accumulation of experiences in totality of who you are and where you have been and they are held together in energy form.

Now you will have different experiences from other people. You will have knowledge through experience of different situations and how to deal with them. Say you have learned forgiveness. It may have taken you many, many experiences or lifetimes to achieve this understanding, but you have learned. Now you are able to teach compassion and tolerance. So you are now in a place to help someone else.

Someone else may want to experience forgiveness

and have an opportunity to forgive. It may be that you may have had many lifetimes to experience forgiveness in many ways, but now you are ready to be given the ultimate test of forgiveness. To experience this you would have to put your physical experience into a place that would allow you an opportunity to feel deep pain or sadness or sorrow to then allow yourself the opportunity to forgive. The person who is now learning to understand compassion, tolerance, and love is now in need of a master or a teacher who will show them how. So you agree that you will allow yourself to be given an experience that allows you to show forgiveness so that it becomes part of their experience just as a parent would to a child who has not experienced life.

The parent leads by example showing the child how to react or how to "be" in any situation. So if we have agreed to this in spirit, we now agree that if we are all aware of this, the lesson will not be as well understood, for the lesson is not the knowing but the searching for understanding. When you reach the point of acceptance, understanding, and forgiveness, you move your consciousness a step higher. You raise your energy and shift into the spiritual energy whilst still in the physical. That is what we are all here to do – to raise our consciousnesses in the physical until we become the essence of spiritual values and understanding in the physical.

Once we have mastered that, then we move consciousness through the physical and a whole new experience begins. We are becoming masters of the physical environment. We are able to do what then would be classed as impossible. We would be able to be in any place at any time and be aware of it.

Lynn Hooper

At the moment our focus is in the physical, and we cut off the spiritual until we access the experiences that allow us to join the consciousness through the evolved energy we are gaining through our experiences. It doesn't matter whether you believe any of this or not. The fact is, you are in the physical having these physical experiences. It is your choice whether you want to access consciousness here. When you pass over, you will then be connected back to source and will be viewing or looking at your accumulated experiences here. You then get to choose the next experience that will help you access spiritual understanding, and you may choose a much harder experience to then question the understanding or meaning of life that then leads to anger and confusion here. Remember: you have cut off and deliberately chosen this lesson. And you have to go through those emotions until you finally ask, "What is the point of this? Why am I always struggling? Why is life so difficult? Why do bad things always happen to me? Why am I so unhappy?"

All these questions and many more start coming up, and you then have a choice to either be angry, to live in denial, or even to blame everyone else for your misfortune, or you can seek understanding through questioning these experiences, which brings you to go within and ask until the answers are shown to you. Sometimes the greatest teachers are the people who choose to be happy, to live life how they wish to be, a great lesson for others who are struggling with why is this happening to me. They believe in living happy lives by their own rules, and that is a great basis for encouraging others to live fully also. But remember: everyone is a teacher and a pupil, no matter who you are. I learn something from everyone I meet, how to do something better next time, how not to do something or react in some way, or even to just enjoy the moment.

I recently had a woman book an appointment via text for a mediumship reading. She was very abrupt and rude in her replies, but I did not allow her to move me out of my aligned (with source) vibration. She then did not show up for her reading, and I sent a polite text saying I hoped she was OK as I hadn't heard from her and that she could rebook if she needed to. She replied a day later without an apology, just saying she was ill. I thought that was it, but a day later again, she texted me, asking if she could book in for another reading.

She was still rude in her manner, and every date and time that I sent to her for an appointment she said no to. Now I felt a little ruffled. Part of me felt angry and wanted to tell her how rude she was and that actually I didn't really want her to come to see me for a reading! But instead I asked her to send me times and dates that she was able to make, thinking she wouldn't reply.

But three days later, she sent over a list of dates. I agreed to the booking, and on the day, she called to say she would be late and wanted directions. As I was talking to her, she thought she realised where she was and abruptly cut me off mid-sentence. I was now feeling stressed. I wanted to say, "How dare you treat me like that!" But something in me felt empathy for her. She was so unhappy, and I wasn't going to reflect her misalignment back to her.

Instead I sat down while I was waiting and tuned into spirit, asking for help to get me through the reading.

I heard a man's voice say to me, "Be gentle." I often hear spirit tell me that when there is a gentle or emotional person about to come for a reading, but to say this to me about this rude lady was a bit of a shock. When she arrived, I ignored all her bitterness, and as she sat down and told me no one had ever been able to read her before I said, "Well, I hope you recognise your husband in spirit who is waiting to tell you how much he loves you!" At that, her world crumbled, and she cried what seemed to be a year's worth of tears, using up my whole box of tissues that I had just put out.

She was carrying so much pain, guilt, and anxiety that the only way she could cope with life without breaking down was to be rude and abrupt so that she didn't have to deal with anything or anyone else. She left lighter hearted than when she had begun, with a sense of relief and purpose again. I learned that day that it is not about anyone else's actions, but your response to them that matters. Being rude to her would have moved me out of alignment, and I would have been feeling as unhappy as she was. Instead I chose to hold my connection. I stayed true to myself and related only from my aligned perspective or vibration. She chose to relate to me from that same vibration, and it gave her space to let all her pain flow without being judged.

They say love is blind, and what that really means is a person can do no wrong in the eyes of someone who loves that person unconditionally. Can you imagine what the world would look like if we all held each other in a vision of unconditional love? No matter what you do in life or how far into the depths of darkness or depravity you go, source unconditionally loves you without ever erring from that vibration. As droplets we have left the source of oneness, and if we lose the feeling of the oneness through grief or anger or sadness, it is painful. If we meet someone who has not forgotten, we feel the connection. It feels like home, and as they show us unconditional love, even though we may not be capable of returning it at that time, it connects us, and we release the pain for a little while.

This lady gave me an experience of whether to choose to meet her in her out of alignment state or in a balanced vibration. I chose the latter, and after her reading, I came away in awe of her ability to cope with the tragic and traumatic events that had happened in her life. I had seen strength in her that inspired me as she was in the darkness and hadn't given up, or as Winston Churchill famously said, "If you are going through hell – keep going!" This is what she had done, and that day I believe she found her way back into the lighter vibration of her true source again.

The most important lesson is belief in yourself first by becoming the most important person in your life. You learn your experiences quickly, and you become abler to help others, abler to be happy and share with others, more independent yet still a pupil. We are all sharing these life lessons with each other. So always keep an open mind even if you don't understand something – ask for understanding, and you will then be guided by your guides and angels to the right person, place, or situation.

We Are Not Our Jobs or Our Uniforms!

Another experience of mine came from a young age. I was in school at the age of five, being taught by nuns. I remember suffering cruelty and unkindness, and it took me years of holding that hate before I realised it often came up in my life as instant anger at the sight of nuns. It wasn't until I was in my twenties that I asked one day why people who profess such love for God could be so cruel. Within days I came across a quote by Mother Teresa, who I had not heard of before then. I still have the quote today.

"I am not sure exactly what heaven will be like, but I know that when we die and it comes time for God to judge us, he will not ask, 'How many good things have you done in your life?' Rather he will ask, 'How much love did you put into what you did?'"

Mother Teresa

That quote seemed to change me in an instant. I realised it was not the clothes but the person. Mother Teresa encapsulated all that was good in a human soul in the physical. I realised at that moment I was angry with the person behind the nun's habit, not nuns. So I forgave myself and the person behind the nun's habit and learned my lesson. We are who we are being in this world, not the job, the uniform, or the money we have accumulated. We are here to be teacher and pupil, to learn to understand and forgive, to reach a new conscious understanding that we are more than the physical, more than the focus we are holding. We are more than any religion, creed, culture, or sexuality. We are divine beings born of the oneness, returning to the oneness, and our journey back to the oneness, in part, is being alive in the physical, putting all our experiences that we have learned and accumulated to date into the expression of being who we are now in the present moment.

Interestingly it was another quote by Mother Teresa that got me through another incredibly hard experience, and therefore, ironically, it has been a nun who has been my greatest help as an adult!

A copy of Mother Teresa's "Anyway" poem was given to me by a friend. It was said that it was inscribed on Mother Teresa's Children's Home in Calcutta and attributed to her, but in March 2002, an article in the *New York Times* reported that the original version of the poem was written by Kent M. Keith. I believe it was then found that another version of the poem was circulating the web with the last lines added, which then became known as the "Final Analysis Poem". I found the poem meaningful and helpful when I was struggling to find answers.

Mother Teresa's "Anyway" Poem

People are unreasonable, illogical, self-centred.
Love them anyway.
If you are successful, you win false
friends and true enemies.
Be successful anyway.
The good you do today may be forgotten tomorrow.
Do good anyway.
You see, in the final analysis, it is between you and God;
It was never between you and them anyway.

What's most eye-opening to me as we come here to gather experiences is that I am reminded of an old saying: "The older the soul, the harder the road." And although effectively there is no such thing as an old soul as there is no time in spirit, there is a raised soul so high in vibration that they come back in our perceived time-space reality as givers of opportunities to us. So the next time you notice the tramp, or someone in great suffering, it just might be the master you agreed to have an experience with, even if it is only a passing moment.

Some Questions for You to Ask Yourself

❖ Notice anyone you see in a uniform (e.g., a nurse, soldier, bus driver, policeman, dinner lady, or even deep sea fisherman) and ask yourself, "How do I interpret who this person is by the uniform they wear?"

❖ If that person retires or leaves their job, would you then change your opinion of him or her without the uniform?

The most important part of this exercise is awareness of your own response.

Chapter 9

YOU ARE NOT BROKEN – YOU ARE EVOLVING!

At this stage in our progression of consciousness as a species, our capability to "believe" is far greater in importance than the understanding. For knowledge comes first. You then have to "be-live" and "be awake" to experience thoughts which gain understanding that is the basic tenet of evolution of consciousness and, indeed, much of life. For your experience of anything determines the next experience and the next until you have a whole heap of experiences that make the whole of you. You then get to choose from those experiences, who you want to "be" as a result of those experiences.

For example, somebody who has been brutally beaten as a child can grow up to believe that he or she is not worthy, and live a life of suffering through the belief of the experience. Or that person can decide to use the bad experience to gain a new insight that it was never him or her – it was always about the bully who had a bad experience and gave another a bad experience. Then that person gets to choose to be like the bully to share the experience of hurting others, or he or she can choose to experience another way of being.

You can choose to believe you are worthy, perfect, and beautiful as you are, that no experience is worth hurting another for, and therefore you choose not to be the bully but one who shows understanding and compassion for those who have not gained enough understanding from the experience yet to "be" love and unconditionally available to live in peace. In other words, you have to be an example of love to teach love. You cannot teach love with hate, violence, or cruelty.

A great teacher whose example of that understanding has stayed with us down the centuries was Jesus. When his life was nearing an end, Jesus said, "Father forgive them for they know not what they do" (Luke 23:34 KJV).

That was an example of teaching love unconditionally from one who knew we are all from the one source but at different stages of evolving our own unique souls. He knew that what you did to another you did to yourself. In his teachings from the Sermon on the Mount he said, "Therefore all things whatsoever ye would that men should do to you, do ye even so to them: for this is the law and the prophets" (Matthew 7:12 KJV).

This is often referred to as the Golden Rule, and it means whatever is hurtful to you, do not to any other person.

Understanding this helps you realise that the choice is a choice you make alone based on your experiences in this lifetime. Now if you go one step further and imagine that you have had not just this one lifetime of experiences but many thousands and thousands of times you have gone home, back to the divine intelligence, oneness, consciousness, heaven, spirit, God, or whatever you choose to feel comfortable with, but you have gone home and then come back to the physical to experience yet another aspect that you desire to experience in the physical, imagine the possible accumulated experiences that can occur and now imagine after each experience you get to choose how to react.

If you choose to become the bully again for many lifetimes, repeating those experiences you delay your evolution. If you can choose to be the loving, caring person who knows that to be kind and loving is more important, your soul starts to evolve in the physical realm. You are literally calling your soul or your spirit into the physical realm and rejoining the power of your divine soul into the experience of the now in the physical realm.

A Droplet Reincarnated

Another way to look at it is to imagine you are a droplet of the one source as we have previously spoken of.

When you, as a droplet, rejoin the whole sea, you can still be aware of your unique identity in the one consciousness. If you separate from the consciousness or whole sea as a droplet again, and along the way you meet another droplet and decide to kick the other droplet into the drain to get rid of it, you have just gone and kicked a part of you down the drain, because you are made of and come from the same source. And when you die, you will go back to that same source or sea of oneness and reunite, and then you will see the experience you had with the other droplet (people in our lives).

And you will say, "Ah, I think I will now see if I can meet that droplet or other person I kicked down the drain last time and do it differently this time." The other droplet or person will also be viewing the experience from his or her unique perspective, and so the process of reincarnation comes into our experience. Now that you understand this, you have to realise all your accumulated experiences become the evolution of your conscious awareness of who you are, more than just the physical, and your accumulated experiences – when given the choices that you had – open your heart or soul, open your mind, and open the gateway, or become closer to the divine realm through which all is possible.

When you are awake because your experiences have woken you up through your choices of kindness, compassion, love and we say this – that these are the conditions of evolution because the divine realm is the ultimate power which is unconditional love, it is practically realised then, that to immerse yourself and work in that power is to open the potential. So now you can open the door between consciousness and the unconscious.

The divine realm is a constant. It never changes in its ability to realise itself but that is the key to understanding. It is about waking yourself up and knowing that you can access the power that becomes the potential for you to be the best version of yourself. You have a proverbial foot in both the physical and the divine realm. You choose to access them – the divine through your raised awareness of who you are and then recognise there is limitless potential, because to access the soul you can access divine power in the physical realm by focusing in both fields. You can them perform what many class as miracles. You become the one who can walk on water, the one who breathes life back into the departed. This is someone who walked the earth many years ago; he had access to both fields of matter and miracles.

Raising Awareness of Who I Am

Think about yourself as the droplet from the ocean that we have talked about previously and ask yourself the following:

❖ Am I separate from all the other droplets or (people) that I share this earth with?
❖ Can I be unconditional and stand in my own knowledge, understanding, and power, asking nothing of anyone else even when they have hurt me?

From this place of understanding, you will cease to judge and condemn and start to teach by your example of unconditional love shown to all without exception. You will then be on the shore of unconditional love as you raise your own vibrational connection.

Chapter 10

YOU CANNOT DIE

We have discussed your journey up to now as a droplet that is a part of the whole sea of oneness or divine consciousness, a droplet that has reincarnated into the physical again and again. What we are saying here is to be able to re-emerge into the physical you have to come from an eternal source – the dimension of the divine consciousness which is unconditional, eternal love. Now that's a game changer when you now understand that no matter what happens to you, whether you die of a disease, an accident, murder, or have your life taken away from you, as a droplet of divine consciousness, you go instantly back to source or pure, positive, unconditional love and re-evaluate what happened. You then choose to come back again if you wish to have another experience of your choosing with others. Armed with this understanding you now realise you cannot die. Your droplet or "soul" or unique you, will choose another physical body to incarnate or re-emerge in the physical.

We could stretch you a little further here and say that you don't actually have to start as a baby. You can create an adult body. Remember the divine consciousness is unlimited, it is only our beliefs that are limiting but we digress here and shall stick to the point. You are an eternal, energetic vibration of pure, positive, unconditional energy or life force that cannot and will not ever, not 'be.' In other words, you cannot die.

There but for the Grace of Unconditional Love Go I

Years ago when I was discussing reincarnation with someone, they asked me if I would like to know who I was in a previous life. I instantly said no, because I didn't want to know. Maybe it would have been good, but what if I had committed a crime such as murder. I would then be carrying around the stress or guilt of what I had been like previously, and I had more than enough troubles going on in my life to have to carry that burden as well.

Although I now understand there is no time in spirit, and therefore everything is happening all at once, in my physical life I did not want to put my conscious focus on something that was out of my control and could do nothing about.

My life now is about the decisions I made before I reincarnated that would serve me in this physical lifetime. Imagine if I had been the murderer in the last lifetime, and now I wanted to address the balance. Maybe the person I murdered (remember the droplet that was kicked down the drain last time) agreed with me that when we went back, he or she would help me address the balance.

So you see, if we now realise and understand that we cannot die, that we can only keep evolving in consciousness, we can look at people who have done us perceived harm and show them the same unconditional love that we are all shown no matter what. Then we will be consciously choosing to move forward in our own personal evolution of consciousness as we are now working in the power of the oneness. It is important to recognise here that whilst we are talking about being unconditional with everyone without exception, you are not seeking to be a martyr, hero, or doormat either. Kindness is not a weakness. You are the most important person in your life, and being unconditional with someone means not judging them but also not allowing them to take advantage of you or hurt you in any way.

You can forgive and act with good intentions to what you perceive as the lowest of all, but I am reminded here of the saying "there but for the grace of God (Unconditional Love) go I," recognising that I may well have been at that stage, and someone allowed me forgiveness as I evolved in my understanding. There are very few of us at the stage of being able to be completely unconditional and I include myself here, but as we strive to understand and put into practice the unconditional aspects of being of non-judgmental and having empathy for others, so our individual consciousness and connection to divinity grows.

Forgiveness Is Easier When You Understand We Are All One

Just recently I attended a funeral, and the vicar taking the service spoke with genuine compassion, expressing his understanding at the sadness of the family's loss, and

I deeply appreciated his empathy. He then went on to talk about the return of the loved one's soul into heaven. As I listened to him quote chapter and verse from the Bible, I could hear his heartfelt desire in the hope that what he was saying was true, that there really was a heaven and that if we believed in Jesus, then we would then be allowed into heaven as well. It is my understanding that you can come from the depths of violence, hate, and depravity, having committed the most heinous of crimes, and still you will return to home to divine consciousness or unconditional love without exception.

Now some of you may feel angry at hearing this, but if we look at this not just from the physical but from the spiritual aspect of it as well, we see a different understanding emerging. We are all part of the oneness or the eternal sea of consciousness. We are not separate from each other, and a part of you resides in every other living being, including animals and innate objects if you go to the complete understanding. What that means is that whatever you do to another, you do unto yourself. Part of the murderer (droplet) is in you, and part of you (another droplet) is in the murderer, as you both come from the sea of oneness and you will both return at death to combine into the sea of oneness. You will be conscious of each other's unique identity, but you will be merged.

When you are in the physical and you access the source or oneness and show compassion, tolerance, or forgiveness to another person, you give them access to that part of you that is raised in vibration which resides in them. By giving them access to that unconditional love, you allow them to feel that love which they have been denying in themselves. It will be as if you have turned a light bulb on inside of them and even if you don't see the change in them in this lifetime, it is now part of that person's experience, and when they reincarnate, which they will choose to if they want to consciously evolve, they will come back to learn how to be that light for themselves so that they then can teach others their understanding, and the cycle continues.

Now when you understand you are helping yourself by helping others, forgiveness can be seen in a different light. Humanity can then start to evolve consciously as a whole when we understand the basic concept that we are all one.

> When another person makes you suffer,
> it is because he suffers deeply within himself,
> and his suffering is spilling over.
> He does not need punishment; he needs help.
> That's the message he is sending.

> – Thich Nhat Hanh

Now in the physical, we can see that we are eternal, and we can look a little closer at death from the spiritual point of view.

Your personal evolutionary stage dictates your life right now and how much access to divine consciousness you are allowing to flow into your daily experience of being you. So now on a practical basis, I would ask you to stop for a moment and consider the question, who am I in this moment of now? I am in this mortal world, defined by my mortal body, yet within I am the immortal presence of the divine essence that forms and creates all of life without exception.

Now just imagine if you had the ability to step outside your physical body. Just step out of it for a second and stand next to it. Your physical body would slump lifeless to the floor, lifeless because the soul is that which enlivens. You are still connected, and it is only when you choose to disconnect completely that you leave the physical body behind. You do this by exiting the thought trail that serves to complete the physical reality. When you stop sending the intent to be physical, the physical body dies away in linear time. If you are still standing next to your body after you have just stepped out of it for a second, the body is lifeless but not dead. It is connected to you via your thoughts, which are a part of you – your essence or soul. So now if you, your essence, can now move freely away from your body, it would be akin to you in your mind being able to float about wherever you choose. You are conscious that you can move about, but you are also conscious of the higher power that you are connected to. This is where you see the reality of who you are, for you don't just float about meaninglessly – you are aware that you are being spoken to or communicated to via the thoughts and energy of the higher sentient intelligence that is still a part of you.

Now if you decide that the physical world is the whole of your existence, that it is about paying the bills and making money, enough to survive and enough to never feel poverty, if this is enough, then you shall not know the extent of who you are, not in this lifetime. If, however, you decide, even for a moment to ask with intention, Who am I, you can momentarily glimpse the best version of your existence. What am I talking about? I am talking about having the ability to go within, connecting to the oneness and what feels like an all-encompassing moment that shows everything and is gone.

It is like watching all the films you have ever watched in your lifetime flash in a moment. You know, yet you are unsure how it is all know in that moment. These are the divine glimpses that are shown through the portal of the mind senses, created by divine connection.

You cannot *not* be connected to divine intention. You are the oneness, but you have chosen to incorporate the physical essence into your reality. Now you can choose consciously to remember, or you can stay asleep, locked in the illusion that the physical body you inhabit and the physical world you live in are your only reality. I can tell you it is not so. The illusion of the physical is created by the whole oneness which you are a part of. You are now experiencing this in a moment of divine awakening. Choose to realise you are more than the physical. Explore the idea that somehow you already know who you are, that you are now discovering how to incorporate the physical aspect of your own self into the wholeness of the oneness. The illusion is about to disappear if you go within and then reconnect, for you are now back to your original form – it is the source, and part of you that you are now awakening to. As you connect, you are opening the possibility for your higher self to touch your soul here in the physical.

Complete This Exercise

The Bridge to Higher Self: Meditation

I would ask you to stop for a moment and consider the question *who am I?* in this moment of now. What is my purpose or my direction? These are the questions you are taking to your higher self as you journey to meet in the higher vibrations of unconditional love.

If you are able to, ask a friend to read out the mediation for you. Or maybe you are part of a group and one person could read the meditation aloud for the group.

If you are doing this alone, then you will have to do your best to remember the journey. It may take a couple of attempts before you remember the way completely, but with practise you will get there.

- Get a pen and paper ready for afterward to make a note of your experience.

If you have never done a guided mediation before asking for support from an angel is often a reassuring way to ease you into the relaxed state needed to make deeper connections with source. Start by using these questions below.

- Ask an archangel to join you, such as *archangel Michael*, who represents strength and guidance.
- Ask your archangel to stay close and guide you so that you may know and feel their presence with

you. Relax and let go, trusting in the route you are going to be taking under their guidance.

- Find a quiet, comfortable place where you will be undisturbed.

- Close your eyes and take a few deep, slow, breaths in and out and then allow your attention to drop to your heart area.

- Now as you breathe in, visualise the petals of a flower opening up, growing and expanding or a wheel spinning and expanding, and as it does, feel your heart expand out like rays of light.

- Just settle into it and sense the love and compassion which now flows through you, filling your whole body with bright, white light.

- As your heart energy grows, you may become tearful or feel a surge of emotion as you open up your energy field. If this happens, relax and just release it and let it go.

- Carry on taking a few more deep breaths in and out and relax into the rhythm of your breathing. As you feel your body relaxing and sinking into your chair, take a deep breath again.

- Visualise a warm, gentle current of air gliding underneath you as you lie deeply relaxed.

- Let yourself go and, with ease, glide along with the lightness you feel.

- Now in your mind's eye, visualise a path stretching out before you. It takes you through a wooded glade dappled in sunlight. The birds are singing as you walk along the path, and you can see a stream flowing gently by.

- Looking up, you see open fields and meadows stretched out before you leading on to a bridge. Looking past the bridge, there is a beautiful building, shimmering, full of energy and light.

- Walk over the bridge towards the building, and as you draw close, notice the doors. They are large and clear like glass; you can see the glow of bright light coming from inside as the door opens effortlessly and you walk through.

- You feel relaxed as the bright light fills you with peace as you walk through the building. You can see seats at the front. Slowly walk up to the seats and sit down. Relief fills you as your whole being is immersed in the light.

- At peace and full of love and gratitude for being surrounded in such powerful energy, you become one as you join the vibration of light getting brighter and brighter.

- Ask the question *who am I?* What is my purpose and feel your words drift into the light.

- Feel you whole body expand in the light and feel the power of the light as it melts into every fibre of your being through your whole body, which is starting to glow with energy. All you feel is joy.

- Stay in this energy for a while and ask your higher self to become known to you. You may see a colour or hear a sound or even see a person. Notice what the person is wearing. How tall are they?

- As the light brightens, hold out your hands in front of you. Very gently a gift is being placed in your hands. Look at your gift and remember it.

- Feel appreciation for the moment and start to become aware you are moving back into your seat.
- Thank your higher self for connecting with you as you say goodbye and leave your seat.
- Walking back out through the glass doors of the building into the warm sunshine you continue through the meadow.
- Walk over the bridge and back on to your path, through the wooded glade.
- You can hear the birds singing as you come back into the room and into your seat.
- Feel your feet on the ground and the weight of your arms and legs in your chair, and you are now starting to open your eyes.
- If you are in a group, then take turns in discussing the gift you were given and any relevance it may have to the questions you asked at the beginning of the exercise.
- If you are doing the meditation on your own, then get you pen and paper and write down everything you can remember.
- Think about feelings, thoughts, colours, smells, and anything else that you can remember that occurred. Then look to see any connection to your questions you asked at the beginning of the meditation.

When I first did this guided meditation, I saw a Chinese man dressed in robes from the eighteenth century. He represented a time of great leaning for me, and I felt an instant connection with him. Your higher self can present any image that you feel comfortable with (remember: there is no need of a physical body in divine consciousness) and will show you an image that you feel most comfortable with and will having meaning for you.

My Chinese man represented the pathway of understanding and knowledge from the divine consciousness that I was waking up to. I was also given a crystal ball, and at first I had no idea why it was given to me.

It took me a long time to realise that it represented the pathway I was deciding on. The way was completely clear for me as I had choices that I could take, and if I looked into the empty crystal ball, what I was looking at what was a crystal-clear pathway that I could create from my heart. It therefore represented my ability to be able to choose whatever my heart desired at that time.

It turned out to be the life I am leading now, which is being a medium, counsellor, life coach, and author which I had no idea I was going to be doing at the time!

Chapter 11

JOINING THE PHYSICAL BODY TO SOURCE CONSCIOUSNESS

When think of your ability to move outside of yourself, outside of your own mind into your original energy form, it then begs the question, how am I being this external form? Who am I, part of or aware of the physical, yet in another state of being – being part of a different energy or awareness? In this state, you can then move into a new consciousness. Technically it is new to you in this moment of recognition, but it is not really new, as you already exist in this field, though you usually exist in this field outside of your awareness or conscious state.

Now you are aware or "becoming" awake, we can now tell you that this altered state gives you access to yet another consciousness, that of humanity, the totality of humanity, for humanity is made up of individuals exactly the same as you but in differing states of awareness. When you become aware, you are able to access the divine potential of the oneness through any other sentient being, even animals.

It takes a raised vibration to do this, to be able to access that level of consciousness. It is not mind reading but being able to feel and see through the senses of another how they perceive the reality of their own world. This is how the spirit world, or your loved ones, angels, and guides, communicate with us. Although that is a strange concept, remember that there is no differing particle in a physical body of human or animal, only the access to awareness of who you are in the moment of now.

Experiencing Individual and Collective Consciousness

So we have reached a level of existence where we can experience our consciousness on an individual basis merely by being aware we are more than the physical body. When we are able to move in and out of our own energy and become conscious that the physical restraint has been removed, then we can feel into human consciousness that is collective and realise we are all one. You are now beginning to experience the oneness of divinity and by moving into divine power you access the collective consciousness. You can then experience every other person's energy field (e.g., you can move your own energy and become merged into another energy).

When you are raised enough in consciousness, you can move your energy into a different place fairly quickly, but the overriding factor here is how evolved your own spirit or energy is. When you are being unconditional love, you are in divine energy, which means you are giving yourself access to transport your mind energy with awareness in human consciousness (collectively). If you have not developed the level of unconditional love and compassion within you, you will not be able to move out of your energy in the next conscious moment.

So taking a break or breather here, if you want to evolve and become more than a physical being whilst in the physical realm, you have to learn to – for want of another word – mind transport or access divine energy to move your own energy into a different consciousness or energy field, and to summarise, you can only mind move when you are working in divine energy.

Awake in a Dream

When I wanted to go abroad, I was concerned about the area I would be staying in and whether it was safe. I asked my guide to show me the area I was staying in. A couple of days later, I went to sleep and then became aware I was conscious or awake in a dream. At this stage of my development, I would not have been able to move consciously to view the scene, so the easiest way for my guide to help and reassure me was to connect with me in my dream or unconscious state.

There was warm air rushing over my arms, and I looked down to see mountains ranges at night. It was light enough for me to see, but I was aware it was night. I was so close to the top of the mountain I could see the uneven surface of the rock and even touch the surface if I reached out. I was elated as I realised I was flying over the area I knew I would be staying in when I went abroad. I was so happy that as I looked down, I could see the whole landscape flying beneath me. I left the mountain ranges as I was still looking down and flew into a massive expanse of sky. I then suddenly realised I was miles up in the sky, and there was absolutely nothing holding me in the air. The moment I consciously thought this, I started to drop like a stone. I immediately lost consciousness as though I had fallen asleep, and everything was gone.

When I woke up in the morning I then remembered the dream. I say dream, but I know that what I had actually did was move my conscious mind into the divine energy, travelling into the oneness of all that is. In that moment, you can experience any place anywhere in the world, because there is no physical restraint. You have moved your consciousness into divine consciousness. This is mind moving out of the way, and the soul is taking over. I was in soul energy and out of my conscious mind. When I became conscious of the physical aspect of restraint, I immediately went into the mind and out of soul.

When you can manage to stop the mind from holding the physical restraint, you can them consciously mind move whilst being awake, or what's called *lucid dreaming*. To clarify here, lucid dreaming is generally described as having a dream that you are awake in, but have no control over the outcome.

I drove past that exact same mountain range when I was abroad that I had flown over when I was asleep. Even now, when I remember that dream, it is not a dream. It is so real I can take my energy back into that moment, although it is only a moment (the moment of being in both fields as I realised I was in spirit but consciously aware I was a physical being). In that moment of being between, the link between the two parts of my consciousness and unconsciousness were in touch, and I became aware of being part of the energy or oneness.

That waking moment was incredibly powerful, and every time I think back to that moment, I hold the exact details in my mind as though I am in that moment again.

Understanding Your Source

We have placed focus on raising your conscious awareness of your spirit or soul or life force being the driving force for your physical body or the enlivening force to help you raise your understanding so that you may also be challenged in your next phase. What we mean by that is, if you decide you want to know more, then challenging your beliefs to date is the only trigger to help you broaden your depth of understanding.

Conscious understanding is a belief that you are more than a physical body, that the physical body is merely a vehicle for the soul to act out or play out its field of vision in the physical realm. Remember: you are not the single, alone life force you previously imagined yourself to be. You are the dynamic duality of spirit and physical. So breathing in life means breathing the energy of the physical into the physical body. This then becomes a sensory digest of information that joins the spiritual or source of you. Now we have a blending of energy. The spiritual senses with the physical senses.

To be awake and conscious of the spiritual element of your life force using your breath to inhale mixes the two fields momentarily. Continue deep breathing and as the body relaxes and takes in oxygen, the cells capacity to translate and transmute becomes deeper. Raising consciousness is about combining the physical senses to spiritual life force. You are literally breathing in life particles and expanding your understanding into the oneness. As you start to move your energy in breathing, so your own life force expands into the consciousness of the oneness.

Feeling and Seeing through the Senses of Divine Consciousness

There is an expanded awareness that comes with completely letting go and breathing into the life force of your senses and experiencing duality breathing. One of the greatest connections I made with duality breathing happened when I was sitting completely relaxed in my garden. It was a beautiful summer's day, and right next to where I was sitting there was an incredibly beautiful, peach-coloured rose. I was in awe of its beauty, and in my joy I felt my whole body relax into a deep sense of peace. As I looked at the rose, my focus moved in to noticing the softness of the petals. They were curved and soft, and as I looked deeply into the rose with such immense joy, I could feel myself getting beautifully lost as my energy drifted. I took a deep breath and started to feel the energy of the rose as one with me. Lost in that moment without focus on the physical or spiritual, I felt my whole life force start to expand out as if touching the energy of everything around me. I could feel the vibration of birdsongs and touch the leaves on the trees in this expanded state. It is something that moved me beyond words. I had experienced the physical through the eyes of source or unconditional love.

Complete This Exercise

Duality Breathing

This is an exercise that takes focus and practise but is worth the patience and persistence if you practise regularly.

The importance of this experience here is to focus on a living energy of nature. You can use the focus of a flower in the garden as I did, or you can focus on a tree, a blade of grass, or even a potted plant indoors. It doesn't matter what the nature focus is as long as it moves you into a feeling of deep appreciation and joy at its presence of existing with you. Once you have found your nature focus, sit quietly with it when you know you will be undisturbed.

- Start by closing your eyes and taking a deep breath in and out. Breathe deeply and fill your chest cavity to capacity with air, hold it for a few seconds, then slowly breathe out feeling any tension in your body leaving with the air.
- Breathe this way two more times.
- Breathe deeply again and open your eyes. Now focus on your living nature object.
- Look at the texture of your nature object. Study every intricate detail of its colour and shape. Notice how it makes you feel as you appreciate every piece of its beauty and form.
- Keep breathing deeply and on each breath imagine you are breathing in the life force of it. Feel the energy joyously combining with yours.
- Take it even deeper and let your mind go. Drift into the presence as if you were breathing in life itself seeping in and taking over your senses in this moment.
- Allow your energy to expand out and feel the area around you. The trees feel close; birds singing are one with you. The warm breeze and the bright blue sky is blended into you. Feel the immense peace of the oneness.
- Hold for a moment and then come back into your breathing. Feel the presence of your body and focus back at looking at your nature object, becoming aware you are back in your physical environment once more.

Through the Eyes of My Guide

When I challenged my guide one day to prove what he was saying, I got more than I bargained for! He was sharing his experience of a particular planet in the solar system, and I asked him how I could believe what he was saying as I had no knowledge whatsoever about the planet he was talking about. The next minute as I was channelling his words, I felt myself drifting into seeing the star he was talking about through his eyes. I felt myself moving over the surface of a cold planet, and I could see and feel clouds and gases which I was almost part of in a physical sense, as though I could just step down onto the grey dust, yet completely able to be one with the gas or cloud without my body. It was such a shock to be there in both the physical and non-physical at the same time, and the power I could feel was so overwhelming I panicked and brought myself straight back out into my own awareness again. I have never questioned his authenticity again after that, but it gave me a huge insight into how we can merge and become one with the source that is us when we are in a physical body and also the part of us that is still existing when we have left our physical body.

Some may term that "remote viewing," which can also be called "mind sensing," which is an experience where you can move your conscious mind into different places without the need of a physical body and see the events or picture of a place, but I use remote viewing in readings to see past and future events, and I know I specifically move my focus into my third eye to do this, so this was different in the sense that I was aware I was not using my third eye. Instead I was merged as one with my guide and consciousness. I could feel the expansion of life and connection with all things – I had touched briefly on the energy of the oneness and it was breath-taking!

Being Grounded Physically

Something that has made me think about the joining of our physical reality to that of the spiritual consciousness is that whether it was connecting with guides, loved ones, looking into the past or future through the third eye, or remote viewing, telepathy and lucid dreaming, the one thing every experience I have ever had all have had in common is I am always aware of my own connection to the physical realm. I never lost touch with that physical part of me no matter what I was experiencing even on strange planets with my guide!

This is the structure that is now joining the spiritual consciousness to ours. We are staying grounded and allowing ourselves to merge from our physical perspective. We do not need to do anything other than stay grounded in our own energy fields and then expand our own consciousness to meet the larger, more expanded version of ourselves, that of our higher self.

Chapter 12

HIGHER SELF

What Does the Term *Higher Self* Mean?

Our higher self transmits the inner globe of light, our soul tune, note, or vibration that is us in spiritual terms into the physical. We then reflect our source, oneness, divine consciousness, God, inner globe of light, or soul out into the physical world via our physical bodies.

Our Blueprint

We have been incarnated many, many, many times. Like an amoeba splits and divides, so our unique soul can keep dividing and reincarnating. We hold the blueprint of the whole within us, and within the whole we retain all parts of our uniqueness that forms our higher self. We have access to that higher self through going within and connecting such as in meditation. Each lifetime we reincarnate, and then when we die or move out of our physical bodies, we go back to source, where we are then able to define a part of us that we feel needs more time in the physical to gain experience. We then move with that sole part of our energy into the physical and into a new body and family, or the same family, to experience a new life whilst the other part of us resides in spirit (the focus of the higher self).

Your higher self is able to communicate with you independently, so it feels like a knowing or wisdom outside yourself when in fact it is your own wisdom garnered by your experiences residing in the oneness or source as your higher self. It feels separate because of the differing vibrations. We are in the lower vibrations of the physical whilst the higher self is in source or pure unconditional love which has the fuller picture of who we are and our incarnation in the physical at this time. You are able to communicate directly with your higher self and with other people's higher selves even when they may not be aware of it or you are not conscious of it. This takes the form of conscious or unconscious telepathy.

Telepathy

Telepathy is generally described as the ability to communicate with someone mentally without the use of words or other physical signs.

Conscious telepathy is the ability to communicate with someone mentally without the use of words or other physical signs and to be conscious that you are communicating with the person.

Unconscious telepathy is the ability to communicate with someone mentally without the use of words or other physical signs and not to be conscious or aware you are communicating with that person.

Deeply Attuned to Love

Higher self to higher self, communication is your deepest intuition, your knowing, and your connection with the source of your higher self, the omnipotence of the "I am", or the divine intelligence that is you, the one and the same you that is divinity expressed in this moment.

A client who is a nurse was sitting with a patient waiting for him to go into theatre to have his operation. The man was very anxious, and the nurse sat and talked with him, trying to calm and reassure him. They told each other stories, and the nurse even managed to make him laugh. She wanted to tell him it would be OK, yet something stopped her. She sensed somehow that he wouldn't come through the operation and thought, "Well, I can't tell him that! That's no comfort!" And at that exact moment she heard a voice in her head say: "Tell me that when I'm on the other side!" She thought no more of it as they were called into theatre. The man was conscious during the operation, but whilst on the operating table he started to slip away. Realising the man's critical situation, the nurse put her hands under the gown onto his shoulders and held him gently as everything was being done by the medical team to save his life. Sadly, he passed away.

When she retold me this story, she was distraught, even though medically everything possible had been done to help him. She questioned whether or not she should have held him and whether there was something more she could have done in her capacity as a nurse. We discussed her role, and even though she could have assisted the team, it would not have been done any differently; it just would have been her instead of another person carrying out the same procedure. Nothing would have changed the outcome. She had since found out that the man knew he had only been given a few weeks to live even after the operation, and it would have been a potentially painful and slow death.

We discussed that the man had knowledge of this before he went into theatre and knew at a soul level that he wasn't going to come through the operation and whether that knowing was the effect of his thoughts on hers that she had picked up on. The man knew that she was doing everything in her power to help him and alleviate his fear, and it turned into a soul communication, or what some people term *telepathy*.

As this was a deeply emotional experience, the nurse was working in a pure, unconditionally loving energy, and in that state of alignment with your true source, you can join the thoughts of others at a soul level even if the other person is not aware of the communication.

The Unseen Existence

To explain this further, no matter who you are, you are (as I have discussed in the previous chapters) part of the oneness that we are all a part of. The whole oneness or sea of consciousness that we all originate from and go back to that exists eternally in unconditional love. And in that unseen existence, you are still a part of it, and only a fraction of the whole of you is focused here in the physical reality.

Every single being on the planet is also part of the

whole residing in that unconditional love and intelligence. So when you are deeply attuned to that love, you can speak to other people who are residing there.

This is the same as mediums who listen and talk to guides, or even when you have communication from loved ones who have passed. The only difference is your guides and loved ones are focused in the eternal consciousness, and we cannot attune to that frequency so easily on the whole whilst we are in the denser vibration of the physical. But if both of you are in the physical and either both of you or just one of you is tuned into the frequency of the divine intelligence, you can talk to that person's higher consciousness, or what is called the *higher self*. It is your unique soul print and different from everyone else's, and even though we are all one, we are still unique in expressing who we are and our accumulated experiences. If you are both attuned to that higher frequency, then you are linking to each other's soul energies or higher selves and speaking together telepathically, higher self to higher self, and you can understand and hear the communication without the need of words, which is what happened to the nurse and the man waiting for his operation who answered her unspoken thoughts.

The ability to do this is strong, particularly in family members. It starts off as a knowing or sensing. We often "sense" when a loved one is in danger before something happens or as it happening.

A few years ago my daughter was out riding, and I had a strong urge to call her, but she didn't reply. Later on that day, she told me that she had fallen off her horse earlier, and whilst she was still in mid-air, her mobile rang, and it was me calling her! At the time I had sensed there was something wrong through that deep intuitive knowing but hadn't telepathically heard her. As the years have gone by, I can now use that stronger telepathic ability, which is a clear hearing of words from others. This doesn't mean you can listen to everyone's conversations in their heads, but you can tune into the energy of loved ones and other people and speak to them just like the man did to the nurse.

Developing Your Telepathic Ability

Have you ever thought about someone, and then the telephone rings, and it is that person? That is you linking into that soul energy of the other person and feeling his or her thoughts. As you develop this ability, you move into a conscious capacity to actually hear the words as they are spoken in the other person's thoughts. It takes practise and deep connection to the higher self to do this, but it is something we can learn to develop over time with practice.

Complete This Exercise

Starlight Breathing Meditation

From ground to sky to light and back

- Find a quiet place to relax undisturbed.
- Close your eyes and breathe deeply several times.
- When you are completely relaxed, move your focus to your third eye, which is in the middle of your forehead.
- Imagine a beam of light stretching out before you. Do not reach for it. Just relax and allow it to come to you as you breathe deeply again.
- Once the light has reached you, allow it to fill your very being. Feel it drift down, filling your whole body.
- Now move your focus to your crown chakra, which is at the top of your head.
- Imagine the top of your head like a window that has opened and allow the light to focus upwards towards the sky.
- Now push the light from within you out through your third eye and the top of your crown chakra at the same time.
- Imagine the light expanding out through the walls and ceilings of the room.
- Now bring your focus back to your crown chakra and send the light up through the ceiling up into the sky, pushing it up through the clouds and up into space, touching a star of even brighter light.

- Breathe deeply and think of someone who is important to you or who you care very much for. Imagine that person's face smiling and send a feeling of loving energy to them. Feel how powerful your love for them is.
- Hold that feeling of love for a few seconds and then drop back down from your starlight to the sky and back through the ceiling and back into your body.
- Allow the light to gently recede and bring your focus back into your body.
- Wiggle your hands and feet and open your eyes slowly and come back into the room.

Keep practising this and notice if the other person acknowledges or says that you came into their mind. A client of mine that I taught this exercise to came out of this meditation, and her mobile telephone rang with the person she had just sent the love to, saying he'd just felt he needed to call her!

Chapter 13

MASTER TEACHERS

Collective Consciousness Can Have a Broken Heart

As we gather collectively, so the raised and not so raised form together. Remember the cycle of teaching and forgiving that lights up another person as you allow him or her to feel that deep connection with source shared in the moment of forgiveness. Well, in each level of consciousness, we have *master teachers* who would share their love and connection to source with us to light us up as a whole.

Examples of some master teachers through the centuries who have done this include the following:

- Jesus of Nazareth
- Mother Teresa
- Diana, Princess of Wales

These are master teachers whose hearts touched millions of lives. They were loved because of their unconditional love and kindness, and we felt their connection to source in us when they showed compassion to all without exception. When they passed, it broke people's hearts. It was a mass heartbreak and an opportunity for us to feel their connection to source through them as that light within and then look to raise it in ourselves.

Many people have mentioned recently that a lot of celebrities have died and that it had become noticeable that they were passing one after the other in a relatively short space of time. They were starting to ask why it was happening and what was going on. These celebrities are teachers affecting those who followed their light, and they gave the collective consciousness of those followers an opportunity also to feel the loss of connection with source that they had and then look for it within themselves.

There has never been a better time to start moving our own unique consciousnesses forward. There is a shifting of the earth's gravity fields, and the solar eclipse is almost complete, meaning the darkness that has shadowed the earth is now making way for the stronger lighter particles. Our own energy has raised this life force to shine upon us. We are calling through our souls' desires for change. Whether you are conscious or unconsciously aware, you are asking for a better existence. And the more who are listening and calling, the more source or divine consciousness answers, and the soul is brought in proximity of the source-energy fields. That said, it is now up to each of us individually to raise up our consciousness to fully allow the consciousness of who we really are to merge into the physical as one with us.

Chapter 14

MULTIDIMENSIONAL LIVES

We are having many lifetimes all at once. I have often told clients that you are living in multidimensional universes, and if you are tuned into the universal energy, not only will you be aware and feel this lifetime's up and downs, but also you can feel the highs and lows of another reality you are living in. If you are highly sensitive and tuned into the soul energy, you can become aware of your own self or consciousness being alive in another reality; this has an up- and a downside. If the life you are not fully conscious of or aware of living is working out well, it can make you feel good, but if you are struggling or, say, for instance, you are homeless and your soul is calling out in pain for help, the part of your soul here can recognise this pull of sadness and be affected by it. You can wake up feeling sad or even depressed as a result of this other life playing out, and you may have no conscious knowledge of it here.

This may sound like a real pain. As if I haven't got enough troubles, I now have to feel or know myself struggling somewhere else, and quite frankly, I don't want to know, as I can barely cope now. That is a valid point until you start to realise that there is a reason you are becoming aware. You can help yourself; in fact, it is incredibly important to be aware that you can change your life for the better in another reality by making your life here better. Imagine you are living the worst life ever here, and you are calling out for help. You in another reality then becomes aware of the call and starts to send positive energy into your life here.

The part of you that is being successful is sending you the help you need. Let's face it; this is you, the part of you that needs help. Why wouldn't you help yourself? Whilst this is part of our evolving understanding, do not get caught up in thinking you need to fix anything. You do not. The best help you can give yourself right now is the practise of meditating and connecting with divine consciousness. In that raised vibration, you raise your own life force or connection with divinity, and any help you need in another lifetime will be sent through your guides and angels as you join together in meditation.

The reason you are becoming affected by your other realities is because you are waking up. You are not stuck anymore in the material entrapment of life. The individual part of you that is being reflected into multidimensional universes is starting to wake up and join the dots or piece together the puzzle that this one physical lifetime is not all there is. In fact, the physical is not even the true reality of who we are so much as a vehicle for us to lay out, or act out, our dramas or experiences so that we might know ourselves. In other words, we are starting to recognise our true identities as source or universal life force where we cannot die. Death in one lifetime is meaningless when you realise you are already existing in many, many other dimensions at the same time. You are merely pulling your conscious focus out of this moment and allowing it to be in other realities.

Getting back to how we can help ourselves here, by even reading these words, your soul has answered your call. You have started the first step into evolving your own consciousness. You are breaking new ground here, leading the way to humanity waking up, which takes each one of us individually to light the path for the whole. When you know you are more than this moment – this material, physical piece of you – that you are awake now, but not in other realities, you immediately seek to make yourself aware in other realties, for when the whole of you is awake, the whole of you starts to create a little miracle. You are free from the bondage of time, physical presences, and limitation. You are aware you exist in multidimensional lives that are occurring simultaneously, and when all of you has caught up with yourself, the ability to move your focus from one reality or life becomes a new beginning of time travel, moving your consciousness into each lifetime. Part of you is already doing this as you would not have drawn this understanding to you. Part of you is already calling to you to wake up. This part of you already knows itself and has let go of fear and ego.

Chapter 15

ULTIMATE PRESENCE

Whilst we have spoken already about collective conscious-ness and how you can connect into it, it is important to remember you are unique in soul and being also and can get caught up in the emotional lives of others. It is easy to do, and we ask you at this point to stop and savour the very moment you are in now.

Being present and mindful ironically leads to being out of mind. In other words, when you bring presence of who you are being in the moment into your experience of now, you immediately start to move into the soul's domain, for eventually the senses take over and peaceful thoughts that calm can be the guiding factor to letting go of the mind.

Complete This Exercise

On the Shore of Life

- Sit quietly somewhere you will not be disturbed.
- Take a few deep breathes in, hold for a few seconds, breathe out, and relax.
- Close your eyes and think of the ocean.

- You are awake. You have a memory of the ocean; you may see it in your mind's eye. It is a nice picture.
- Now close your eyes, take a deep breath in and out, and hear the ocean, hear the waves hitting the shore back and forth for a few seconds. Now listen to the gulls as they pass in the distance. They fade and you feel the sun warming your face.
- Now you feel the sea's water warm over your hands as you dip them into the sea. You look up and see the horizon, the sky touching the water. You take a deep breath. You could be anywhere you choose, but you choose the moment to be.
- Be still. Feel the calmness, the power of oneness. You are home in the soul of eternity for a moment.
- Now hear the sea on the shore and then move back out into the presence of feeling yourself sitting back in your chair or whatever your body is in contact with.
- Open your eyes.

We ask you now: what is the difference now as you look around the place you are surrounded by in the physical? What is the difference between what you are looking at and feeling in the physical and that which you have just left, the peace of the ocean? We tell you now: you are back in mind before you were giving your mind over to your soul who took your conscious thoughts and allowed you to feel into the presence.

You have not moved in the physical, but your mind moved into the energy of the soul. It is a valuable exercise to help you connect within until eventually you hand the whole experience over to your soul or higher self.

Your mind moves out of the way, and the experience is taken into the divine realm where there are no limitations. Your presence is everywhere and nowhere until eventually every action, every molecule of your physical being, can be moved also. There is a thought, is there not?

- ➢ How did it feel to be still?
- ➢ Were you able to achieve stillness?
- ➢ If you weren't able to be still, ask yourself why not?
- ➢ If you struggled to be still, then think about ways to relax your mind before you do the meditation exercise, such as going for a walk or listening to music that makes you feel relaxed.

Chapter 16

GLOBE OF CONSCIOUSNESS

You have been given a vehicle (the body) to use all its abilities in the physical – to shine, grow, emerge, and be the force of God or oneness within to bring that force into the world around you. This force is the oneness that you are being. You are in a globe of raised consciousness. To break out of the restraints of the physical, you have to have a tool to break free.

You have been given the mind-brain in your physical body to connect within to your consciousness or globe of inner light.

Your inner light cannot be worn away, broken, or destroyed, as it is pure consciousness, or the oneness, and you are one with it. To break free from the confines of the physical, you cannot kick your way out; your physical attributes are useless with that approach. You need to sit quietly in your globe of consciousness and go within. Ask for your mind and body to reconnect to source to allow you to feel divine presence.

This is where the change then starts to appear for the light within starts to expand. Your reality starts to expand. Your physical experiences hold you in one place, but your mind when connected into the soul shows you a different way of being.

When you use your conscious mind to experience truth, love, and kindness, you step forward in your light, and the light grows and grows until eventually all the experiences you are having become one with you. Every kindness or act of love becomes absorbed into your consciousness globe as it expands. Negative emotions and deeds restrict growth of your globe of consciousness as negative energy is a lower vibration, and you confine yourself to a smaller and smaller space until you are stuck with no room to move. This can be changed immediately by your thoughts. Love and kindness will ease the pressure of this confinement of your soul so all experiences have an impact in the moment you are in.

Eventually, when you have mastered many, many experiences and you walk in love and divine presence, the globe of consciousness you walk in does not break but becomes merged into the divine oneness.

It is a gentle transition that is not really noticed, for the journey feels the same; your heart feels the same but just becomes expanded. When you are walking within the oneness of divinity then the universe is the essence of you being. You manifest with ease the things you desire, and at this stage, your desire is to help others to be released from the self-imposed physical restrictions, to help others understand the journey is vast, magical, and more than you can ever imagine was possible. It is the expansiveness of consciousness that you have merged into – there is only love present.

Chapter 17

EVOLUTIONARY JUMP

Eventually all things must come to an end. The difference in endings in the physical and the consciousness of oneness is that oneness never ends; it just changes form. So this is true really of the physical. Your body dies and everyone sees you have stopped being. You no longer exist; your life has come to an end. But in truth, your life is merely moving forward into the next choice of reality that you are about to proceed to, which is of your own choosing upon your return back home in divine consciousness. Only you do not need the physical body. The soul releases the attachment to the body by dissolving the conscious barrier which is the self-imposed physical restriction we have just spoken of. It absorbs you back into consciousness, or rather, it merges your soul, which is a part of the consciousness, back to itself, and every trouble you ever had drifts away. You are held in love so deep you fall into relief and ecstasy.

I talk of going home for that is where you go back to the full understanding of who you really are, the spirit or soul of divinity in an experience or expression in the physical.

Once you have reached this understanding whilst in

the physical, you no longer see death as a loss or ending but rather as a celebration of love, for you go home back to love in its entirety, and you choose the next adventure of spiritual experience.

Now that you understand this in your life right now, how does it make your life better for knowing this? Well, for the start, knowing is merely the key to experiencing. You have to experience being the divine presence whilst in the physical body before you can merge into the collective consciousness that is many other people in their own inner light globes.

When many other people's inner lights start to shine out, when they walk in love, kindness and particularly peace, they automatically shine out their presences in this higher vibrational field and reach out to meet others doing exactly the same. You then have the ability to merge, to join as a unified, expanded globe or global consciousness.

When the many start to collect together in this raised awareness and expanded state, the expansion is quicker and more elevated. The whole becomes closer to merging into one and when collectively each individual raised in consciousness joins together, you start to bring the divine realm to earth in the physical, and that will change your earthly experiences quite dramatically.

Within these fields of energy all things are possible! This is the next stage of humanity, the evolutionary jump into the realm of divinity into the physical, and it is not only worth doing, but also it is essential for your survival as a species, as humanity, as human beings.

Complete This Exercise

Heart-Guided Meditation

Meditate using the sea-globe picture.

Calmly visualise you in your inner light globe joining with other like-minded people. You will literally float away into your merged consciousness for a while, and you will bring the calmness and peace from this exercise into your daily lives.

Relax. Look at the picture below that flows into a circle and follow the directions below.

➢ Relax your mind then focus on the whole of the drawing, following the lines into the centre of the circle and then pulling your focus back out again.

➢ Now focus on your breathing, taking deep breaths in and then releasing as you keep following the lines of the circle into the centre.

➢ Keep focusing on the circle and your breathing until you feel your body start to relax.

➢ When you are feeling relaxed, start to visualise the sea, hearing the waves move with the lines as you focus into the centre.

➢ Close your eyes and keep visualising the lines flowing into the sea still hearing the waves.

➢ As you hear the waves rolling gently on the shore imagine they are now moving underneath you lifting you up.

➢ Imagine the feeling of rising up, as a bubble of warm air surrounds you.

➢ As you drift up you can see other circles of light all around you, glowing and drifting up with you.

• As you continue to lift up drifting over towards the land and fields in the distance you feel a deep sense of peace.

• Send your own joy and happiness of this moment out from your heart as a burst of loving energy rays to all that are sharing the light journey with you.

• Feel the rays from your heart expand out into all the other light energies as their heart rays also join with you.

- Glowing as one, there is a feeling of love and appreciation for all life as you relax and together drift into a higher brighter light.
- Feel the peace, serenity and oneness of the moment and breathe deeply.
- Relax and enjoy the peaceful drifting of energy of oneness as you move back down across the fields, allowing your body to relax, drifting gently back onto the shore.
- Hear the waves gently receding into the distance. Open your eyes and become present in the room again.

You were born with potential.
You were born with goodness and trust. You were born with ideals and dreams.
You were born with greatness.
You were born with wings.
You are not meant for crawling, so don't.
You have wings.
Learn to use them and fly.

– Rumi

Chapter 18

DO ANGELS REALLY EXIST?

An angel's presence is constant. They are your
travelling guide through life and eternity. Through
darkness and light, they will be with you.
Hold your head up high, for you walk
in the company of angels.

Angels – What Are They?

Angels are very highly evolved beings of light existing
in such a high vibration that they are accessing the
higher vibrational frequencies of the oneness, divine
intelligence, God, or consciousness. They are the
highest human equivalent of life in astral terms, and
the consciousness of humanity is accessed by angels.
They are completely integral in humanity to each
individual and each individuating, incarnate human
soul.

As pure consciousness, angels don't have the physical
traits of the body or the ego and can traverse both the
spiritual and physical world.

An Angel Is Part of Every Single Person's Soul or Inner Globe of Light

When we think of angels we think of celestial beings far removed from ourselves, all-knowing, all-loving, without judgment or condemnation, so far removed from some of the practise of humans that they feel otherworldly. Yet their otherworldly qualities are not inherently different from our own. They share our love and compassion for others, and it is their quality of non-judgment, non-violence, and non-hate that pulls us towards angels. We feel safe in their company no matter who we are or what we have perpetrated in life.

Angels are here for us unconditionally. They protect, guide, uplift, and support us no matter what.

What Can You Call on Your Angels For?

- ❖ Guidance and support in our everyday lives
- ❖ Healing
- ❖ Protection
- ❖ Contacting loved ones in the spiritual realm

Reasons for Contacting Your Angel

Are you a developing medium, a healer, or someone who simply wants to improve his or her life by having knowledge of his or her angel that supports and guides in everyday life.

All contact with your angels comes from within, but you will then find a way of expressing that communication via, channelling, writing, music, healing, art forms such as painting, and any other way that you have been inspired to work, including humanitarian work or just simply needing help with everyday situations involving family, friends, colleagues, or work.

Your angels are developing your inner guidance system with you to help direct you to the pathway that your heart most desires, such as resolving conflicts or easing your resistance to problems so that solutions can be found.

How Do You Contact the Angelic Realm?

The best means of contacting your angel is through meditation.

You can build a strong connection with your angels in meditation. Journeying within you start to sense and feel your angel's connection. It will be an experience of inner peace and bliss as you relax in their uplifting energy.

How Do You Know Your Angel Is Listening to You?

Very often we doubt the validity of an angel's help because it is easily missed in the subtleties of life. If you are asking for help from your angels, then be open to receive their help in any form.

We are here to develop our experiences here on the earth, and an angel will not take your experiences away from you, but the angel will support you unconditionally no matter what. It isn't until you ask for help from your angels that you allow the full benefit to flow to you.

Your angels will always love guide and support you

unconditionally whether you realise it or not, but in your asking, you are expecting help in some form, and in your expecting you move into a state of openness and allowing.

Trust your intuition or inner knowing that you can feel or sense. Don't ignore the phone call you feel urged to make. Go with the feeling of changing your route into work or wanting to suddenly reduced your speed when driving. Stop and take notice of the subtle signs that are being shown to you. It may feel strange, and you may not realise why you are doing things differently, as you cannot see the end product, but trust in the guidance you are receiving and follow where angels lead.

You are never alone
always an angel rests gently by your side.

Your Unique Pathway

Angels know the path you have chosen in your physical life, and they can move through the lower frequencies or vibrations in the physical to connect with us in our dreams or as a vision. They can guide us to someone in the physical who can help us, and they can even manifest as a person to aid someone in distress.

A while ago an angel sent someone to me as a chance encounter in a car park, and although it was a brief meeting, I believe the man found peace from someone the angels knew would ease his anxiety. It all started with this question:

Can You Tell Me the Way to Heaven?

A very strange thing happened to me yesterday. I had just arrived at a beach car park, and as I got out of my car, a man who was walking by quite fast stopped suddenly and turned to ask me: "Can you tell me the way to heaven?"

I was so surprised that it took me a second to collect my thoughts, as we were next door to the Haven Inn, and he had been walking past it.

He had a tanned, careworn face and such deeply searching eyes. I felt I had heard him correctly but my logical mind said, Ask again, so I asked him, "Where did you want to find?"

He replied clearly, "Heaven. Do you know the way?"

I looked at him and thought, Are you really asking me this? He was staring so intently at me, waiting for my reply, that I decided to just answer his question and said, "Bless you; it is in your heart."

His face changed to one of surprise and uncertainty, and I wasn't sure whether it was because someone had answered his question or the reply itself. He became serious and said, "But how do I find it?"

I answered, "You feel it." I put my hand on my heart. "It's within you every moment." His face softened, and tears started to build in his eyes.

He said, "I nearly died two years ago and I should not be here now."

At that moment I was joined by my husband who interrupted the man as he walked in front of him. The man, realising the conversation was over, looked at me with deep intent again and asked, "But do you think I will go to heaven?"

"Without question you will go to heaven," I replied, smiling.

His face lit up, and a wave of peace and happiness seemed to find him all at once in that single moment. He suddenly thrust his tanned arm towards me, and I could feel his overwhelming gratitude in the intensity of his handshake. He then made off as quickly as he had appeared.

Although a bit surprised at first at the encounter, I realise that our angels and guides will never miss an opportunity to help us.

Whether you are being reminded that loved ones are close, or whether you need help with a situation or question as that man did in the car park, know that your angels will always be there to help, guide, and support you in your life.

Your Twin-Soul Angel

What Is Our Twin-Soul Angel?

Our twin-soul angel holds the overview of our inner globe of light, or soul, in the higher vibration. It is like holding a tune and keeping it playing. Our vibration is the note or tune.

Your angels never question, doubt, or lack belief in you, for they know and see the broader picture. They see the human form, but they also see the spiritual form, the part of you that resides in spirit. They see the pathway you have chosen, and your twin-soul angel, the most refined part of your own energy, will have formed a unique bond with you that holds your place in consciousness as you then choose to experience the physical.

Your twin-soul angel is like your celestial shadow; you cannot be without your twin-soul angel being a part and together with you. So as you move, so does your angel. As you sleep, so does your angel, although you are connecting in the spiritual realm with your angel when you sleep and you chat about what is happening and what you would like to achieve.

You then move back to focus on the physical, and when you wake, your angel retains what you have discussed and helps you when you are having a difficult time with something, for they know what is really going on and how your heart feels and what lesson or experience you are giving yourself.

Even though you can be in the most difficult of situations, you and your angel both know that it is of your choosing, and your angel is your supporting hand in both physical and spiritual terms.

Ask an Angel for Help and the Angel Will Respond

I asked today if the angels had a message they wanted to share and these are the words I heard them say to me:

An Angel's Promise

"In the stillness I shall meet you – and you will be free."

Those angel's words reminded me of the times in my

life when I felt the load was too heavy for me to bear, when I struggled to get through each day. I spent some time every day in meditation, and the relief to be free in those moments encouraged me to keep going.

The angels are encouraging you to take time out of your day and sit in silence, allowing them to draw close. They will call to you and ask you to join them in the stillness, pure and unconditional; they will shelter you from the storms of life and will fill your whole being full of happiness and joy, free from pain and hurt. In that moment, you will be free.

Complete This Exercise

❖ To connect with your twin-soul angel, sit in your meditation space that you have created, or find a quiet, comfortable place where you will be undisturbed.

❖ Say the "This Day" affirmation below either out loud or within to bring your energy into alignment with your intention to connect with your twin angel.

This Day

This day and always, I trust the angel who walks
through life with me as my guide and shoulder to cry on
This day, I put my trust in the angel that
walks with their wings around my shoulder –
my angel who is always by my side
This day, I hand over all my cares and worries
to my angel as I connect in the silence.

The guided mediation below is something you will
have to practise slowly. It maybe that you will only be able
to remember the beginning as you meditate and that is
enough to start you off.

If you practise every day, eventually you will be able to
walk the journey in your mind to meet your angel.

Now follow the guided meditation below to meet your
angel in a place of tranquillity and peace, trusting they
are with you as your journey into the place of silence to
meet them.

Meditation to Meet Your Twin-Soul Angel

- Close your eyes and breathe in deeply and out
  slowly. Repeat four times.
- Now listen for the gentle sound of water cascading
  down into a pool of crystal-clear water nearby.
- Move your focus to your third eye in the middle
  of your forehead.
- Breathe in deeply and out slowly again. Listen
  to the gentle flow of the waterfall and enjoy the
  relaxed feeling of peace within as you watch the

water dance and sparkle in sunlight as it falls down into the pool.

- Now move your focus down to your chest area and imagine your inner globe of light glowing as the sparkling waterfall gently spills over, pouring down into it. It spins effortlessly as though afloat in the water, and you are filled with a bright light that now starts flowing into your arms, hands, legs, and feet, then surging up into your chest, up through your neck, filling your head space, and then connecting up into the universe as one.

- As you focus back into your third eye, you notice a change as though looking into a mist. You see the outline of angel wings. They embrace you, and you feel safe and loved.

- This is your twin-soul angel rebirthing into your soul as one with you.

- As you walk together, the waterfall pours down, glistening and sparkling in front of you. You can see through into a tranquil oasis of colours and sounds as you walk through.

- The crystal-clear pool of water emits a harmony as if playing musically in tune with you as you sit next to it with your angel. You feel absolute peace in this moment.

- Notice the love you feel as you share your concerns with your angel.

- This is your time together. Ask whatever you want. No request is too much for your angel to handle. Share all your concerns and leave them with your twin-soul angel.

- When you feel you have talked for enough time, thank your angel and walk back through the waterfall.
- Waving goodbye, you feel a deep sense of peace and contentment.
- You feel yourself drifting back into your inner globe of light again in your chest area.
- Feel the weight of your body once more. The grounded connection you have to the physical earth as you move your feet and hands, bringing you back to the room as you open your eyes.
- Take a minute to reflect on your journey with your twin-soul angel and take the peace and contentment you feel with you through your day, knowing all is well.

I have guided different people through this exercise, and each person has a different experience, depending on what is needed in his or her life.

Some feel as though they have received healing from their angel, and some have seen a vison that has guided them to make a decision in their life; other people have had a feeling of immense love to let them know they are not alone.

Whatever you come back feeling from this guided mediation is what your angel knows will be the best help for you at the present time.

Chapter 19

WHAT HAPPENS WHEN OUR LOVED ONES PASS OVER?

Loved ones in the spirit world draw close to us on many occasions in our lives, but there are times when their communication with you is so profound it changes your experience in the physical.

No one ever passes alone. I have said many times to people that an angel is with you from the start of your journey from the spirit world into the physical. They are here from your physical birth and throughout your whole life until you are exiting your thought trail and letting your intention to be in the physical diminish.

They are aware, before you are in the physical, of your intention. Remember, there is no time in the spirit world, and they can be in a multitude of places but also aware of exactly where you are and the exact moment you ask for their help. They are already drawing close to you before you depart. Although unseen, they will be with you no matter what. They also use a part of their energy to allow loved ones to draw close to you in the days before you pass.

The story below was shared with me – as a question, to begin with – during a reading I was giving, and it did not surprise me at all that the lady had been chatting with her husband in the spirit world in the days leading up to her departure.

There is such comfort brought to those getting ready to pass. Knowing their loved ones in the spiritual realm are ready to greet them makes their transition so much easier, knowing they will be there with them at their passing. It is, however, free will and the desire to speak with loved ones that are the overriding factors.

If you are scared at the prospect of death and are trying to cling on even though you have asked your soul to step back into spirit, the angels will stay with you.

Even if you have no faith whatsoever in angels, spirit, or an afterlife, it makes no difference. Your angel will be with you when you start to cross over, guiding you into a place of peace until unconditional love fills your heart and you realise you are home once more.

Visiting with Loved Ones from the Spiritual Dimensions

Just recently, a care worker told me about an old lady in the care home where she worked who kept saying that her husband had been to visit in spirit, and they had talked about the plants he was growing and how the sun was always shining and how their cat was still getting under his feet.

She'd said she had also visited in spirit with him and walked in beautiful forests and woods filled with brightly coloured bluebells and flowers she had never seen before. There had seemed to be such a glow of happiness about her as she'd shared her stories every day that, although the care worker thought she may not be fully present anymore, she had been glad that the old lady was happy. One evening, the care worker noticed the old lady seemed a little downhearted. After the worker had asked her if she was OK, the old lady had replied, "I couldn't be happier. My husband has said we are going home tomorrow, and I wanted to say goodbye to my friend, who I will miss."

The care worker had still thought the old lady was a little confused and had told her everything would work out OK, and her friend would understand. She'd thought no more of it, said goodnight, and left her.

The next day at work she'd found two staff members clearing out the old lady's room. They were sorry to tell her that the old lady had passed away in the early hours. There was a letter by her bed, written for her friend down the hall, saying goodbye.

The whole story made the care worker come to me and ask if the lady's husband really had been visiting her from the spirit world. I told her with certainty that our loved ones would make themselves known in the easiest way for us to feel secure.

This lady's husband had known she would be overjoyed to see him, and he'd made her preparation to depart to spirit that much easier by allowing her to see and feel the spirit world with him before she joined him.

Never doubt that spirits are with you. Their love for you never fades. Your angel has the ability to bridge the gap between the physical and the spiritual, and their energy allows our loved ones to draw close to us when needed. In the case of the old lady in the story, there was a need for the husband in spirit to join his energy with his wife's in the physical to make the transition easier. This joining of energy allowed the old lady to enjoy the time in spirit and remember it to ease the way for her to move into spirit without fear.

Sudden or Traumatic Death

Now, when you understand that it can be a simple transition, there is also another element to this – in the case of traumatic or sudden death. Although we may think in the physical that a death was sudden or without warning, we can tell you that it is not the case in the spiritual realm. All is known as we go back to this no-time theory. Everything is unfolding in the now. There are no mistakes, and no one is ever overlooked or dies alone.

Even if you could not be with a loved one as they passed and think they died alone, they did not. As we mentioned earlier, their twin-soul angel will be with them at all times as they transition from the physical into the oneness, or divine consciousness.

We can tell you that, even when there is a very traumatic death in the physical, your angel and loved ones are already aware before the incident.

The soul of the person in the traumatic passing is moved or lifted from their physical presence at the moment of physical impact, and they feel no pain or suffering. They are literally held in the arms of angels and feel nothing but peace as the angels surround them in unconditional love.

What Happens to People Who Take Their Own Lives?

A person who takes his or her own life is met with unconditional love and feels a deep sense of peace as they are also held at their passing in the arms of angels. Angels do not differentiate. We are all part of the oneness, and we all go back to the oneness. Remember, you are a droplet of the oneness incarnate. A part of you resides in every other person, and they also reside in you. It can be no other way. No matter how you pass, you are met with the same unconditional love, without exception.

Upon their return to love, a person who has taken his or her own life will have exactly the same choices as we all do. They see the whole picture as they merge into the oneness, or divine consciousness, and will evaluate how they lived their life and will base their next experience in the physical on what they want to experience next.

As part of soul groups, they will often reincarnate – as many of us do – by choice, back into families with the same people from our last experience, creating an opportunity for everyone to experience another lifetime together in a greater understanding as a result of the previous incarnation.

I am reminded of the words *never judge another*, for in any one of your last experiences of life before you reincarnated again, it could well have been you that took your own life, and maybe you have grown through many, many more experiences and are now able to teach others. Always, it is love that keeps you together as you share and teach each other through your experiences.

Our Soul Family

Each of us living has a soul family that we are connected to in the spirit world, but we are often so busy in our daily lives that we do notice their helping hands.

Soul Families are the loved ones who have walked through life many times before with you. They will have travelled on many journeys with you and fought many battles with you also. They are the ones who help us to fulfil the experiences we chose before we came to the physical earth plane by guiding us from spirit when we are having difficult days.

Have you ever felt down and a loved one who has passed to spirit has popped into your head, and you remember something about them that makes you feel better or inspired? That is a member of your soul family supporting you. It may be someone we recognise, like a family member or close friend, but it may also be a feeling that comes over us. You may not always recognise their presence whilst you are here, but when you go back home to spirit, your soul family are instantly recognisable and will be there waiting to greet you with your angels.

Our Soul Family Groups

Our soul family resonates at the same frequency, or vibration, as us in the spiritual dimension, meaning they are closest to us on the vibrational scale.

Our soul groups are made up of the people who are on either end of that vibrational frequency. Just like the tuning of a radio frequency, which we spoke of earlier, so too are your soul groups made up of members that are on the edge of each end of that vibrational scale. Some will be emitting a higher frequency at the top, and others will be just emitting enough to come close to you at the lower frequency of the group.

You incarnate with other members closest to your vibrations in the group, who are the family members, and then you have those moving up to meet your vibrations, who are often the family members with whom you are going to have deep and meaningful experiences that will challenge you to grow in frequency.

As you incarnate with these family members, you can be any relation to them, such as mother, father, brother, sister, cousin, or in-law. You can choose to be male or female in any relationship, so you could have been a mother in your last incarnation and choose to be a father this time around. You are unlimited at source and are free to choose.

You are making choices and agree together what you are going to next experience with the other soul family members. It is a cycle that moves as you grow in consciousness, and the lower vibrations rise as the group moves together as a whole.

Remember, you and the person you incarnate with are still residing in the spiritual dimension as the main part of you, or the higher self. Effectively, what I am saying is that part of the person who you *think* has died and gone back home is also residing in spirit with you as your soul group. It is only a part of you that is reflected into the physical. The main part of you is eternally residing in the spiritual dimension.

The other interesting understanding I have been shown is that your thoughts here will dictate what the spirit world looks like to you. We have the levels of light, or the vibrational attraction, we have spoken of, but you will only be in your own soul group with other people on your vibration level, since you gravitate to them automatically. You will not mix those vibrations or move into vibrations that do not match yours as you do in the physical. This, again, is the reason for the physical to be a leading light for experiences which you do not attract in the spiritual realm.

Soulmates

How Many Soulmates Do You Have?

Soulmates come in varying forms in our lives. Some are partners, lovers, even friends or family, and some you may only meet briefly on your journey through life, but there is no mistaking the feeling of unspoken love from soulmates. They understand you when no other can. They need no words; their presence is enough. You don't need to ask if someone is your soulmate – you feel it in your heart.

We have said that, in spirit, we can choose to be either male or female and also choose what relationship we have with each other when we incarnate into the physical realm. We can spend many lifetimes in our soul groups being brothers, sisters, mothers, fathers, sons, daughters, and friends.

As result of these changing roles, each time we come back to the earth plane, our soulmates can often be found in other relationships. Even though we tend to think of soulmates as a love relationship, that love takes many forms, and it is quite normal for the soulmate to not be romantically linked to you in this lifetime.

This is often why we can have more than one soulmate, some romantic and some purely on a vibrational level of love through the soul energy.

If you've ever felt that intense feeling of connectedness with anyone who you are not romantically linked to, then they are someone who is on your soul level, or vibration, including another soulmate.

Love takes many forms, and someone who is always there for you will be a soulmate whose heart remembers the bonds of love from previous lifetimes. No matter what form of relationship you have in this lifetime, that love never leaves our hearts.

Meeting Your Romantic Soulmate

A soulmate's time with you can be brief, but their love will live in your heart forever. Can we meet someone, fall in love, and carry that love for the rest of our lives, even though the meeting is brief and you never see that person again?

When we come across a soulmate in life who does not become part of our lives with us, we can feel it our whole lifetime, wondering *what if*?

I met a lady who had a single post card as a reminder of a love that she'd held a whole lifetime, after a week in which she fell in love with a man who she'd never seen again.

His love for her was evident as he came through from the spirit world to explain how he had carried the same love for her, too, and watched over her now.

It was evident that this was a soulmate relationship as relief, sadness, and joy mixed together to bring tears to this brave lady, who left with the one spark of hope in her heart that she had not lost her love, but would reunite with him again one day.

Her words were to me were that she would not make the same mistake twice. Next time around, she would not allow others to dictate her life, a decision which had led her to feel the loss of his love her whole lifetime.

That was a beautiful experience, to see the courage grow in this lady's heart as she learned through her experience from her soulmate, and she found strength in herself to do things differently next time.

Meeting your romantic soulmate can be one of the best and worst times of your life.

I have always understood that the people who give you the hardest lessons often love you the most. My guide has always said, "Who better to give you the worst experience of your life than someone who loves you?" This means that it is better that you learn a hard lesson from a place of being loved, rather than from someone who is not able to feel the same depth of emotion and not give you the deeper experience needed for your growth.

Soulmates can appear at different times in your life.

- ❖ They can be present with you from birth.
- ❖ They can come in halfway through your life.

❖ They can appear when you are going through a particularly difficult time in life.

❖ They can touch your life momentarily.

Two Notes in Perfect Harmony

Soulmates are the closest link between an incarnating droplet of soul and a sea of oneness on the physical mountain ledge that splits.

Although a droplet can scatter into many parts and drift into new existences, a soulmate is the closest vibrational match of that droplet to you. When you are close to a soulmate, you can feel that alignment, since you are both equal in vibration.

You are two notes that are in harmony, or are perfect in pitch and tone, resonating as one. Soulmates can make you feel completely at peace, but equally take you way out of your comfort zone as they bring their separate, learned experiences – the ones that you are seeking to experience.

Soulmates do not come to necessarily give each other an easy time. They are here to be teachers as well as pupils. Often the greatest love stories have the most painful heartbreak.

When a soulmate's love touches your heart, you share the flow of source and double the feeling of being at one with divine consciousness. Your inner lights shine brightly, merged as one, but when one goes out, you feel as though you have been left in the dark.

Having No Belief in the Existence of Life after Death

In the physical, we see death as an end to our lives and our existence. But if you look at it in spiritual terms, you are merely deciding to move your conscious focus out of the physical and back to spirit, where you then become aware of (and join up with) your soul groups and angels.

If you have no understanding of this in the physical, and you believe when you die you cease to exist, then you may be surprised to know that the moment you pass you will automatically recognise your soul group members and your angels.

It will be like greeting a loving family member or dearest friend. You will regain the whole picture, and you will then have an opportunity to assess all your earthly experiences, if you choose.

I would say here that some who have absolutely no belief in the afterlife, who hold on stubbornly to that thought trail, are not lost and will realign into spiritual understanding as the physical thoughts eventually start to feel out of truth with their energy or spiritual vibration.

I have mentioned before that as you cross into divine consciousness you are constantly surrounded by highly evolved energies such as your twin angel, guides, and other soul group members, all of whom are affecting your vibration, raising it to a higher level until it starts to seep into the vibration that is you. That is when the physical thought trails start to weaken, as they serve no purpose and feel out of balance with who you are now becoming at a vibrational level.

If there is resistance still with the passing – and what I mean is if there is a shock to the person from the sudden passing, or a feeling of realising they still wanted to be in the physical – then I have been shown places that look very much like our own hospitals.

There are individual beds that have a bright array of colours within the light, and the person is immersed and surrounded in these beautiful, colourful rays which have a vibration of their own.

We draw the exact colours that are needed to heal us to ourselves automatically, only they seem to have an effervescent quality about them and, unlike colours in the physical realm, they have a tone or vibrational sound which emits the healing energy. As you progress in your healing, you can have the form of the body which most do, but it is only your thought trail that is being gently realigned to spiritual vibration. You are able to see the physical world forming around you.

As your physical thoughts trail off, so the spiritual vibration becomes aligned, and as you rejoin the oneness, so you start to see the physical world forming around like a movie playing out on an invisible screen around you. I can only describe it as seeing a place you have created – say, for example, a beautiful meadow fully of brightly coloured plants. At first it will form like a distant, hazy picture, but as you realign, the vison becomes clearer. As you focus upon it, similar to as focusing on a tree or plant, the image starts to get nearer. As you align, it becomes part of your environment the instant you focus on it, and everywhere you focus, it immediately starts to zoom forward. You learn to place your thoughts carefully, rather than create by default.

Imagine it like this – think of your meadow with the brightly coloured flowers. If you see your meadow, and then it reminds you of cows in a field, you will then zoom in to see the cows in the field. That reminds you of a bull, and then he is in the field with the cows next to you.

Now you have lost the focus of the beautiful meadow and are at one in the field with the cows and the bull. You are aware of their presence next to you, their size, smell, and colour as you focus on them.

As you look at the bull so you are instantly focused in next to him, and immediately you think of being somewhere safe away from him, and now you are in the distance at the far end of the field away from bull and the herd. As you think, you are instantly moved to that thought like a flashing light appearing and disappearing as you focus and unfocus until you learn to balance your outpouring of random thoughts.

It is akin to waving a magic wand and things appearing and disappearing, only it is your own energy that is the magic wand doing all the creating.

Once you realise you have the ability to create with the power of your thoughts instantaneously, you are going to want to focus rather than be jumping everywhere onto random thoughts. You have to remember that you are not creating this from the physical realm, so you have a much more expanded ability and awareness to create.

Now you understand that as you align your conscious thoughts into focus, you can immediately see your loved ones. You can listen in on them and feel how they are feeling. You can sit in your favourite chair next to them, and your strong sense of connection can be sensed by them through the love you both hold. You become the ghost, if you like, around your loved one, only you are not trying to scare them, but desperately trying to let them know you are well and strong and whole again.

Ghosts

As we come to this subject, bear in mind there is more than one type of ghost.

Remember, the word *ghost* is just a description of someone we think is dead in the physical, but from spirit, you are just caught up in the physical illusion and cut off from seeing your loved one – who is very much alive, but in their true form.

I have just mentioned seeing the ghost of your loved one, but you can, if you are in vibrational alignment, see ghosts who are people in a different time-space reality. You can be aware of them, yet they cannot see you, and to further blow your mind, you can be the ghost who others can see in a differing time-space reality if they are sensitive to time, and particularly if they are connected to you through your soul groups.

If you are in different timelines, that is the reason for seeing the differing stages of clothes that were worn though the centuries.

We are limited to what we can see through our vibrational alignment, and as such, we are only just waking up to the future ghosts who are much-raised in the light spheres, or vibrational consciousness. As they are a pure energy form, we can see the angels as they traverse the energy fields, but not much beyond that at this stage of our conscious evolution, or our focus here.

Dream States

In your dream state, you reconnect to source and join the oneness. Those reoccurring dreams which are so vivid are you seeing another timeline that you are focused in on from the spiritual realm. I personally have been aware in my dream state of my own death under a collapsing building. I remember becoming aware that I was lying face down on the floor and feeling panic going through me, and as I lifted my head up, I could see a concrete ceiling stretching out as far as the eye could see. It started falling on top of me, and then I abruptly woke up. I realised I had just died in that reality.

Yet, in another reoccurring dream I have had, I am aware of being in the future and a battle raging above me. I stand in another concrete building, but this time at the top, in an apartment. I can see other tall blocks joined to each side of the apartment block I am standing in. I hear an explosion and feel a wave of panic as the building shakes, and I run to the balcony and look out to see spaceships just above me, firing into the next-door block and then suddenly racing off. I hear the deafening noise of the jet fighters thundering in, giving chase.

It is so real I see every gleam of spaceship and feel every vibration of the building as it moves. I hear the noise of my footsteps on the steps as I race down the stairs and into the bright sunlight of the street outside, which is surrounded by nothing other than rubble and a derelict town.

I have asked several times the reason I keep seeing this dream, and I am aware it has something to do with the future of my own timeline, although I don't know exactly when. The reason I am writing this book is that I can feel the direction of my own guide urging me to finish this book, to help others gain understanding as the future of our planet changes and evolves.

Chapter 20

DO CHILDREN GROW UP IN SPIRIT?

I have included in this chapter questions and answers that were given to me after asking about children in the spiritual realm. Sometimes they are complex and difficult answers to navigate through but we have asked and divine consciousness has answered us.

Do Children Grow Up in the Spiritual Realm?

The paramount note here is choices. We have spoken previously that all children are born into the earth's atmosphere through choices. They are guided by their experiences and are taught both in physical and spiritual terms.

The answer, therefore, is twofold. Firstly, there is no time in spirit. Secondly, as there is no time, you can effectively be at any age at any time in a multidimensional life.

If a child still retains their thought trails, they will be settled in a lower egoic energy, which is the unconditional love of spirit slowed in vibration, just as the earth plane is, but not as slow. So in spirit they will be living a vibrational level of slowed energy which will slowly allow them to adjust to being back in spirit. This energy level is not just for children but for anyone who is still holding on to thought trails.

As a child becomes aware he or she is in spirit, which the child does by being held and surrounded in the unconditional love of angels, the child has soul families that join the angels and start to help the child realign.

To realign, they have to start letting go of the thought trails of the physical which no longer serve them. They do this by sitting with masters who hold them in perfect alignment with their own energy.

Whether the need to heal from a physical ailment or an emotional trauma, they will be receiving a master's alignment through the energy that is being sent to them. As they receive this constant energy vibration, the thought trails start to lessen. They are allowed to use the multidimensional universe to visit (this is going to sound crazy) themselves as they were before they passed. They will see that it is only a fraction of who they are, and it is only their focus that holds them in the physical, that the hologram of physical life is created by spiritual existence.

So all timelines are, in fact, being played out all at once and are being reflected by the greater part of ourselves in spirit. Once we pull our focus in spirit out of the timeline, we diminish the thought trails and release ourselves back into the oneness or knowing. So everything is but an illusion created by you and only discovered by you once the thought trails have diminished and then be left behind as we merge into spirit.

How Can a Master Come Back as a Child?

It is the same principle as all who come back. You choose another experience to grow up in; this covers the spiritual realms as well. We have discussed the need for experiences to expand our consciousness to allow divinity access to flow through us in all environments and atmospheres, so as you can see the choices are endless or limitless. Let us say you are a child who has chosen to come to the earth plane and only live a few hours. If, on your return home to spirit having fulfilled your experiences along with your parents who also agreed this with you, you have done what you set out to achieve, you are now back to your original energy form.

We have to understand that knowing is not the same as experiencing. We can be given a complete set of instructions on how to drive a car and learn it perfectly, but without experiencing driving a car, we will never know what that physical experience feels like or if we are even able to drive a car. Knowledge comes first, then the understanding or the experiencing.

As to growing up, remember time is a physical phenomenon; it is not relative in spirit. Although we would like to say you grow up in spirit if you pass to the spirit world as a child, this is not strictly true. You have access to a multidimensional life, and you would not want to block that access off in spirit as we do in the physical.

So you are saying children don't grow up in spirit?

No. We are saying there is a choice, but the choices are in spirit. You can choose to learn access from the masters (or someone who is high in vibration or connection to source or the oneness), but it is not the same as the physical.

How?

A child who comes back to spirit from an embryo to a young adult has the same access to grow. Their experience of coming back from such a short stay in the physical (in physical time) expands their consciousness.

Yes, I get that.

So we do not enter spirit as a child, per se, unless we are holding onto the thought trails.

Ok. So there is a choice?

Always it is a choice but remember we have previously said that traumatic deaths or something that keeps the child's focus in the physical will stay with the child on passing, and we go back to the healing until the thought trail has evaporated, and the child has become aligned to spiritual focus again.

There is no physical body in spirit, there is only energy, and once your energy has aligned, you become part of the totality and fully focused at the vibrational level you are on.

Healing Colours

If a child passes to spirit and has not exited the physical thought trail, they will have healing surround them constantly.

The colours are drawn to them and stay with them. Unlike adults who tend to stay resting in hospital environments, children respond far better to soul group involvement so the other energies of your family members in spirit will be guiding and helping the child to refocus into alignment. Some children are there for a while, and for some, it is an instantaneous transformation back to the awareness of what you would term *complete knowing*, or in the physical you would term *an adult*.

Spiritually they are in full knowing or awareness of the experience. If their focus is strong, they then can come back to the ghost form we have previously described to be with the parents and other family members including animals they were close to. So it is a choice. They will send and receive messages that relate to their childhood experience to their loved ones left in the physical.

You Are Not Limited in Spirit

Your soul is your unique vibration that you have attained up to now as a spiritual energy or life force. So a child when it returns home to spirit is not limited by the physical body anymore and can be their fullest self which is not limited by the physical restrictions of the brain.

Whether you are highly evolved in consciousness or lower in vibration, you communicate from that level of vibration which means you can communicate as what we would perceive in the physical as an adult.

As there is no time, so their focus can move back into that energy on the timeline, yet also be moving forward in awareness of the physical age that we count.

So a child that passed say when they were three will be able to come back at that age if they wish even though their alignment in the spiritual realm is complete, they are merely shifting their focus.

We would add here your guardian angel who is assigned to your soul through those developed experiences together play a huge part in the unconditional love they hold for the child or soul that passes, as they see it, back home. They are always connected to the child and are there supporting and loving them no matter what. Each child will go with their angel back to their vibrational level with the soul family and are engulfed in powerful love. There are no mistakes and absolutely without exception every single baby or child is held in love every step of the way and feel immediate overwhelming peace and love as their angel and loved ones hold them close as they travel home to spirit.

No Child Is Ever Lost

No child or adult is ever lost on the way back to spirit, but they do have a choice where they stop. In other words, if they choose to hold back as their thought trails are strongly rooted in the physical, then angels and soul families surround them in love as they help them adjust into alignment.

Once the thought trails have been exited completely, then they can move forward into the complete vibrational light level they are on, but there is a lesser light vibrational place as the hospitals that we spoke of that create a holding place of love as you realign until your transition is complete.

The confusion here is where some describe some souls as lost or trapped. They are neither. They are held and loved, and they can move freely back and forth from spirit to the physical until they realign. They know where they are, and it is a choice when they move forward.

Ok. So a child can stay a child if the child wishes if they don't exit their thought trails and stay on that level? That still sounds stuck to me!

When you are in the physical and you make choices, you do it with the understanding you have. If something is entrenched in your thought patterns, it can be difficult for you to change your mind, but it is a choice. When you are in spirit, a similar thing is occurring. You haven't exited your thought trail, and you are being shown that there are other ways to be and often children, and adults alike are guided back to see their loved ones in the physical to show them they are not in the physical presence of them anymore.

Often this is done with a discussion, as the angels know how you are feeling as they are connected to the energy of your soul or heart and know when it is the right time to show you where you are in spirit compared to the physical.

Every Decision You Make Is a Choice

You have to remember absolutely every decision you make in spirit is a choice. There is no other way. The reason for the delay is merely the holding of the physical thought trail which is stuck in linear time, and although we say stuck, you are not lost or stuck, as you are freely moving back and forth from physical to spiritual and vice versa as you lose the physical trail. There are realms of light that you can play out the physical connection in spirit.

So you are saying you can grow up in spirit?

No, my child, what we are saying is you are never stuck. If you wish to continue with the physical trail and are not ready to completely lose it, you can stay in the demi worlds or halfway houses of spiritual light. It allows you a closer connection to the physical, and it is a choice to stay there.

Some people have said that when we are in overwhelming grief that we hold our loved ones back from moving forward into the spiritual realms. Is that what you mean?

No, my child. Remember: it is a choice. Although their pain will be felt, it is known to all spiritual souls that not only can you not die; you can never not be with someone. In fact, the loved one left behind is only a small portion of who they really are, and the larger part of them greets the child or adult in spirit as part of their soul's group. There is an immediate awareness of there being no loss. It is only in the physical we feel loss.

If that's the case, why would you want to or choose to stay in a holding place if you could easily move forward to your own conscious vibrational level with your loved ones?

Again, it comes back to choice. There is a differing energy present in a holding level that you can experience. It makes you become aware of the difference between physical illusion and reality of your own energy, so there are experiences being had there too.

So a child can stay as a child in a holding level at the age the child passed and the child doesn't grow up in the spiritual holding level?

They grow up in the sense that they attune to spiritual

alignment that re-forms. It is not a true ageing, as there is none from a spiritual point of view.

But if they are in a holding level?

Time is not relevant in spirit; there is no ageing. That is a physical element only. The timeline ended at the age that was chosen. There are new choices to be made. The child can then return as another child to the family if they wish and would also have been agreed. They may also grow in another realm, and by that we mean, choose to experience a different birthing – one of consciousness rejoining

Every choice is made before you arrive and has been agreed with the people you incarnate with. So a baby who passes back home to spirit is not a baby in the sense that there is no physical body, only spiritual energy or soul that enlivens in the physical, and that energy aligns or goes back into spiritual vibration as it aligns to its true self.

As a child grows up in the physical, all that is happening is his or her focus of spiritual consciousness is slowly developing. If there were no time, the person would be an adult, child, and everything else in-between as it is all happening at once. So, you see, growing up just isn't the same in spirit, as time has no function.

You've said that there are levels in spirit where we can slow time down a little, and also you said there are levels of light where you can play out the physical. What does that mean? It sounds like a place to grow up in!

No, my child. Again it is back to time. There is no time, but yes, you can experience a level where time is created to a level where physical abilities can be played out. The difference is we create time by slowing down the vibration that helps the child to exit the thought trail gently. It is not the same as the physical vibration. It is a different level or vibration that slows a little. It gives a mixed version to the child, allowing a small part of the physical to still be present if their desire is so strong.

They can have a body and do things physically as well as getting healing access to the spiritual realm. If you like, it is a plane to adjust rather than to grow up but to remember who you are.

There is no ageing, only a transition of thought until you align perfectly with spiritual vibration.

Do Children Go to School in the Spirit World?

Can a child go to school there?

Yes, but not in the complete sense you are imagining. They go to gather experience of letting the access flow. They are given light to work with and colour to play and shape. They are healed with the colour and do not exit as in the physical. They are in spirit using some of the physical illusion until it serves them no longer. Always loved ones and family from your soul groups are with the child and always unconditional love is present.

Healing Vibration of Masters

Often if there has been a physical disability, for example, the child or adult is shown how they can choose through their energy vibrations to let go of the thoughts of disability (remember: you do not need a physical body in spirit, but your thoughts create your reality just as they do in the physical).

The physical thought trail or physical energy will still keep creating a disability with you, even though you are free of the physical body. Remember the field of cows and the bull. If you keep focusing on the bull, it will keep becoming your reality, so too will the experience of disability if you hold your focus upon it.

As children and adults are realigning and losing the thought trails, they gather together with a master healer who will be fully present with them, holding their wellness as complete.

The master's vibration can be felt by the child or adult and then attuned to the frequency of the master. This allows them to then let go of the physical thought trail. That is the kind of school in spirit you would belong to. There is no separation, just high-vibrational healing. When the child or adult is ready to accept the perfect vibrational energy that the master holds of them, they align to the frequency, and they become one with spiritual energy and exit their old limiting thought trails. So it is not ABC that you would imagine is being taught, so much as attunement and alignment.

Thank you. I wanted to fill people with love and hope, and I have battled a little with this concept as it doesn't feel very clear.

Your Child Is and Always Will Be with You

My child you are waking up to the knowledge that there is no death. Once that is accepted into your vibration, your grief will cease, and you will never lose anyone, no matter what the experience is, as your connection to the spiritual flow of who you are becomes stronger in your present awareness.

There will come a day again where you will walk back to spirit with your loved ones to see them safely home for yourself, and then you will come back again, such will be the power of your alignment thorough your understanding and experiences that have expanded your conscious awareness.

We want to emphasise in this chapter that death is irrelevant. It does not exist as we are eternal. Your child is and always will be with you, and the understanding that grows within you lessens the grief until you fully accept who you are and the illusionary world you are living in.

Chapter 21

COINCIDENCE AND SYNCHRONICITY

What Is Coincidence?

Coincidence is a physical expression and one that is not applicable in spiritual terms, as all is known, and all is playing out according to your free will. You have decided the major life events you wish to experience in the physical and then you are left with free will. Your thoughts create your reality and are your free will. If you are vibrating on a negative energy that is what you will attract to yourself.

Remember: there are certain life events you have chosen, which could be an illness, poverty, wealth, disability, or success in something, and then you have chosen, together, people who you incarnate with that will give you positive and negative experiences that you wanted to go through. It is then how you *respond* to those experiences that your free will (or your thoughts create your reality) attracts to you your experiences in the physical.

This is similar to the thought trails that need to be exited in spirit, only in the physical you will keep encountering what it is that you are drawing to yourself and may not fully understand the reason it is happening to you.

Some may call it luck or coincidence, but the synchronicity is your free will drawing the energy of like that attracts like to itself, or even more succinctly, the law of attraction draws to you whatever you put your focus on.

Every Thought Is a Living Energy

You have to remember that every thought you have is a living energy in its own right; it is consciousness evolving. As you place your thoughts on something, you are sending out a vibration on that level.

If you think about how many thoughts you have in a day, you can see how crazy your attraction is going to be if you have a million differing thoughts on the same subject. It will become irritating and confusing for you. But if you recognise that each thought has possibilities that can play out in your life, then you are creating a timeline that is beneficial to you.

You are connected to everyone and everything, and if your thoughts become a strong enough desire, they collide or meet with someone else who is also vibrating his or her thoughts on the same wavelength.

As you believe time is real in the physical, you will have to build up the momentum of the thoughts, and then they will start to appear in your life.

It is the linear time that we have created that gives us time to keep changing our minds, and you will then quickly learn the importance of staying focused on what is important to you until one day it shows up, and someone will say, "What a coincidence! You were only just talking about that!"

So coincidence and synchronicity are unrelatable in spiritual terms. They are merely you focusing your thoughts into a place of your own choosing, and be it good or bad thoughts, positive or negative thoughts, they are being created by you through the universal energy that you are a part of and that flows through you. In other words, you have forgotten that you are the omnipotent divine energy that can create worlds, focusing your energy into this physical reality.

Once you realise this, you can create anything you desire if you learn to focus your good feelings into everything you do, for as you sow shall you reap!

Meditation and Manifesting Your Desires

There have been times when I have felt the power of spirit working through me and times when I felt quite alone. Each of those times I was in charge of my connection to source. Source or divine intelligence is always present; it is only when we move out of alignment that we feel disconnected and alone.

Maybe someone said something to you that you found hurtful and created sadness within you. Maybe you failed to achieve what you wanted to create, such as a loving partner, a new house, job, career, car, more money, or good health.

Maybe you are just angry that nothing ever seems to go right! Whatever you are feeling, if it is negative, then it lowers your vibration, and you move away from source. The good news is that you can raise your vibration with practise fairly quickly to align back into the positive energy of source.

Whenever you are striving or rushing or feeling upset, just stop and take a breath. Breathe into the moment and decide that everything is OK. No matter what the situation, it will pass. By breathing in and out a few times, you automatically start to centre yourself into a balanced energy. It doesn't matter where you are. It could be in a queue, at a restaurant, or at a family gathering, staying calm and grounded in your own energy field will start your vibration spinning into a higher energy field, which becomes the law of attraction energy working for you from your deliberate control.

In a calm but higher vibration, you are connected to source, and source creates and delivers to you without question anything that your heart truly desires by your state of allowing or being happy and in alignment with source, oneness, divine consciousness, or God.

Practise meditating, even if you only start with a few deliberate deep breaths in and out each morning. Begin to extend the time each day to a minute, then five minutes, slowly bringing your breath into attunement with the energy of peace you are creating.

In this state, you reach a state of allowing, and things that you previously thought were not possible start appearing in your life.

Daydreaming

The divine source will deliver a daydream in exactly the same way as it delivers anything you are feeling. Everything that happens to us in our life starts out as a thought that then manifests, so wouldn't it be better to choose what you want to manifest in your life rather than creating it by default?

Have you ever noticed that something you keep thinking about keeps reappearing in your life?

I always wanted a red sports car when I was younger, but I couldn't afford one, and everywhere I went I kept seeing red sports cars! My belief in visualising the sports car was easy, so they kept appearing, but as my belief was also that I couldn't afford one, I never managed to buy one. Years later, after I had let the desire for it go, I ended up buying a new one! I had stopped the belief that I couldn't afford one, and the divine source or universal intelligence then delivered to me my desire as I had no resistance to it.

Being Present

Never be afraid to be present in any moment. It is your choice to face a moment and collect the energy, for that is a moment defined – a piece of energy that you place value upon whether it is a collection of memories or the collection of possibilities of what-ifs. They are all in this moment.

So what are you doing with your moment? Are you gathering dust? Are memories holding on so tight there is no room for new moments?

Divine spirit does not judge or condemn. It is the "I am" of all moments. When your moment comes to you to be, you deliver your energy into physical form. You switch into a field so vastly different from the energy of the soul that it can feel as if you are a stranger in the world. Let the influence of love be present, for you are a collection of active energy brought to form by the enlivening of the soul.

Your thoughts really do create your reality. You are a magnet which draws unto you every moment of choice and unconscious choice you make.

Every living thought is a signal attracting the energy of the thought into creation. Each thought is still present with you, but the ones that hold the strongest feeling or attachment bond will be the strongest threads.

When links cross, confusion happens. Be clear about what your beingness is creating. It is your whole being, your whole energy, that pulls it to you. The thoughts that have emotions are the strongest threads, for your energy creates a stronger thread if you weave from the universal life force out of your feelings.

So if you create a problem by allowing it to be, then detach from it, allowing it to pass. Holding on to the feeling creates more of it.

Dealing with Emotional Blockages

Emotional blockages are the past-life stuff we all carry around with us from the moment we are born to old age. They are the difficult childhood, the relationship that went bad, the loss of a loved one, or any traumatic event in your life that affects you emotionally, and as your emotions are your guidance system to all spiritual communication in your daily life, if they become blocked with negative energy, such as hate or anger or sadness, then your ability to communicate is lessened as you become out of alignment with your spiritual link to source energy.

Once you recognise these blocks in your life, you can make new decisions based on your choices to create a happier lifestyle.

Complete This Exercise

Spend a day taking note of what you focus on throughout the day. Are your thought patterns more negative than positive?

If your thoughts are more negative than positive, try the exercise below to help release those thoughts and create more positive ones.

This exercise is designed to look at the emotional blocks in your life that you may not even be aware of and then finding a way through these blocks.

Look at the list below and fill in your answer on the right-hand-side column.

What is making me unhappy? For example, "I don't like my job and I feel stuck," or "I feel lonely a lot of the time."	Your Answer:
How do I feel about changing what is making me unhappy? (e.g., "I am fearful because …") **Where in my body do I feel blocked or unhappy?** (e.g., Head feels fuzzy or cluttered or my stomach feels tense.)	Your Answer:

How can I change this situation that makes me unhappy? e.g. I can change my thoughts into more positive thoughts such as: "I am good at my job" "I am deserving of a loving relationship"	Your Answer:

Look at your answers and make a new column. Then write out the reasons for your answers (e.g., if you wrote in the last box, "I am good at my job," now write the *reason* you are good at your job).

List everything you can think of that makes you good at your job. Now think about how you could bring those skills with you into another job and focus on how much benefit you could bring to a new employer in a new job that you would like to do.

Or if you wrote, "My stomach feels tense," recognise that your anxiety over your unhappiness is showing up as tension in your stomach area.

Every time you feel the tension tell yourself that it is OK for your stomach to relax and let go of any troubles now as it no longer serves you to feel this way. Meditate and focus on how relaxed your stomach now feels and notice any shift in energy as you start to relax. Keep repeating this exercise until you no longer need to.

You can transfer this positive thinking to any answer you write down and soon you will have started a chain of positive thoughts which the law of attraction will reflect back to you in life.

Looking at the Bigger Picture

Now I want you to ask yourself the question:

> If I only had a week to live, how would
> I live out that last week?

Now write down the three most important things that you would want do in that last week you had left.

1. _____
2. _____
3. _____

Look at your list again and ask yourself, "What stops me doing those things now?"

Your answer to this question will give you an indication of how ready you are to start living a more rewarding and fulfilling life for yourself.

Now ask yourself this question: "If I didn't get those things done in my last week before I die, how would I feel?"

Don't be too hard on yourself if you aren't ready to say yes or do any of those things yet.

Give yourself time to think about them and then visualise what your life would feel like if you had done all three things on your list.

Tomorrow is a new day and a new opportunity to create the life you are dreaming of.

Chapter 22

HOW DOES HEALING WORK?

From the words of
divine consciousness:
I don't see you as broken or in need of fixing. I see
only the part of you that is whole and well, so you
too, may see the beauty and wonder of you.

I have never trained as a healer in the traditional sense as some would recognise, such as Reiki Healing, but as a qualified counsellor, life coach, and medium, I have seen and experienced the power of healing at work.

I have always been unconventional in the way I deal with things, and healing has been no different. I once went along to a healing workshop a few years ago to try and learn something about the way healing worked. When it was my turn, I tuned into the psychic energy of the person and could pick up areas of darkened energy. I can only describe what I was doing as feeling or sensing the psychic field. When I scan a person's body energy or aura, I start by looking at the person as whole. Then my vison tunes into the auric field around the person, and I use my clairsentient ability (or clear sensing) to feel the different vibrations or energy in the person's body. When someone is unwell, the vibration seems to stop in the area and shows itself as a darkened area.

At the time, I really wasn't sure if what I was sensing was right. I asked my guide to let me know. The guide confirmed what I was seeing and then added a bit more about troubles that were going on in the person's life.

This was the first time I had ever done anything like this, so I just blurted it out to the person I was working with. The shocked look on her face was apparent as she said to me, "Yes, how could you possibly know that?"

I shared with her that I had asked my guide, and I was then rather curtly told by the teacher that how I was working was completely wrong! Now I am not saying that the teacher was wrong, but I would say that to me, if something works, then go with it. I may have been a little rough around the edges, but I would have enjoyed the chance to learn more. However, I was then put off going any further because of the teacher's remarks. I never went back to any healing workshops after that.

I am not blaming the teacher here. At the time I had no real inclination towards healing, and even though I have been given many messages from other mediums since, saying I should work as a healer, I decided to follow what my heart wanted to do.

I spoke earlier about having abilities from previous incarnations, and I believe I have been a healer many times previously in the physical, and this is the reason I am now being pulled in a different direction. Now that I think back to that experience, I realise it was helpful for me even though I didn't think so at the time.

When I work as a counsellor, I see people who are

having physical symptoms, such as bad backs, who tell me about feeling overburdened with responsibility. Even in my own life, I am writing this whilst healing. I knew that I needed to rest, but I didn't listen, and I ended up breaking my foot and having to rest, which ironically led to me finally writing this book!

In other words, physical symptoms are a result of two things: firstly, they are a reaction to your thoughts, as the law of attraction will bring to you what you are focused on, whether it is good or bad; and secondly, they are also about the choices you made before you came to the physical earth plane.

When I was in the healing workshop, I could see from what my guide was showing me that the lady I was working with was having heart palpitations because of an experience she was going through. In other words, she was reacting to something that was happening in her life. In another experience whilst working with a client, I could see that the light was leaving the client's eyes as the thought trails were tailing off, or they were preparing to go home to spirit.

When I looked into this man's eyes, I saw and felt his connection with divine consciousness. It is a deep, meaningful connection when you look into someone's eyes. They say you can look into someone's soul through the eyes, and I would say that is a fairly accurate description. I felt the man's life force or energy, and I felt the low vibration that happens when thought trails start to tail off.

To understand this feeling, imagine listening to a full orchestra playing music, and then one by one each instrument stops. The last note is the same as the last thought to be in the physical.

To describe it another way, imagine a guitar. Pluck one string and listen to the string vibration ring out and then fade away, and you have the energy leaving just as the soul leaves the body. The physical vibration stretches out the note so you can feel its vibration or stage of life force which is what I did.

Both of these people wanted healing and wanted help. The lady who needed healing could have been helped by counselling and coaching to guide and support her to move into a more positive mind frame. The gentleman who had a difficult illness was having a different experience; I could see he was having the experience he chose before he came to the physical. I knew that he was searching for the understanding of who he was, and often it is in under extreme circumstances that we do the most soul-searching.

The difference between the two of them, in short then, is that one was out of balance because of her reaction to life and the other was having a life experience chosen before he came to the earth plane. Remember: we may choose our life experiences before we incarnate, but we also have free will too.

It is therefore our responses to our challenges that are the differentiating factors. Either person could have a different outcome. For example, the lady could have responded so badly that she created illness within herself and suffered and even passed into spirit.

The man could have strengthened his understanding and belief to such a degree that he only held wellness within him and lived a long life in the physical. It is exactly the reason we choose those experiences before we come here – to learn how to respond and be in perfect alignment with source or unconditional love or divine consciousness or God.

Choosing Illness

Some may say, "I would never choose to have a disease such as cancer or put myself through an accident that would be disabling," but that is exactly what you do if you want to grow your soul's experience.

Remember: from the spiritual realm, this is an illusion created by yourself to give you these experiences, and you know that on passing you will exit the thought trials, and you will not have any illness or disabilities. And if you don't exit the thought trial completely, it is a choice that you have. When you wish to, you will realign completely into well-being. I have said previously that in spirit, masters hold you in a vison of perfect wellness. They do not fight anything and only see wellness, and that is the basis of healing here on earth too. The only true way to help anyone is to hold them in a vison of perfect wellness. The greater your level of alignment to unconditional love you have, the easier it is to allow healing energy to flow to someone asking for healing.

Remember: we know not the experience someone chooses before he or she incarnates, and it can be incredibly difficult to understand how a loving, caring person could suffer to a terrible illness, but it was his or her choice for a reason only he or she knew.

Until we move back into the broader understanding of divine consciousness, the best we can give anyone going through difficulties or trauma is to show compassion, understanding, and acceptance, and allow that person his or her experience.

Or as my guides once said to me when I questioned why I had to struggle through an immense difficulty, feeling I had no help from them, "Who are we to take your lessons from you?"

You are never alone.

Even though it feels like you are alone at times, you are not. You are always loved and supported by your guides, angels, and loved ones in the spiritual realm. They will not interfere with the choices you made before you incarnated. Instead they will do everything in their power to help you understand and guide and comfort you as you grow through the experience and gain wisdom and understanding.

Why are some people not healed no matter how much healing they receive and still pass to spirit?

There are some people who are choosing to go through the experience for a reason. There are some who believe they cannot be healed, and there are some who are so out of alignment that they go down a negative pathway and cannot bring themselves up enough to receive the healing being sent to them.

These are all times when healing is ineffective to halt

the passing. I would add here that all healing helps, even if you think it doesn't. Although you may not be able to change the situation, the loving energy sent to someone either in person or by distance healing will have an effect to a certain degree. It may only be a slightly better feeling in the person who is sick, but it will help ease their suffering a little and that is worth remembering.

Just to clarify here, you can leave your earthly existence, or what we would term in the physical "die" early, before the time you agreed in spirit before you came, but you cannot extend past the agreed time.

You are neither judged nor condemned no matter how you passed back into the divine consciousness.

There is a misconception that some people who have taken their own lives or passed through an act of suicide will somehow be condemned. This is not the case. They have merely moved so out of alignment that they have all but extinguished the light from their souls.

To explain that further, when you feel there is no answer to a problem, you can feel trapped and without hope for a future of happiness, which is the opposite of the divine consciousness. In that feeling of hopelessness, you block the light, or the divine flow to you, by your negative thoughts which are so far away from unconditional love it becomes unbearable. In that state of pain, sometimes the only way to reconnect and feel the unconditional love of source again is to end the thoughts which are trapping you by leaving your physical body.

Although it is heartbreaking for the person left behind

in grief, there is some comfort in knowing that the person who took his or her own life will have been met with such unconditional love that he or she will instantly be relieved of the pain.

To clarify here, they cannot completely distinguish the source of light within them whilst in the physical. We are *all* eternal beings and can never die. They will merely change forms as they move into the divine consciousness, God, oneness, or divine intelligence, and they will be loved unconditionally by their angel and soul family as they make their transition to spirit.

Those who have taken their own lives or pass because of suicide will go through exactly the same transition process we all do. The only difference is that when they reflect in spirit on their lifetime in the physical and realise that they went through those experiences as a choice, they may then choose to come back again in the same circumstances to see if they can gain a deeper understanding of how to connect with divine consciousness in the physical.

How Does Healing Work?

I had no intention of becoming a medium, but my guides knew I had chosen that pathway.

Some people who are working as healers already know that healing is their pathway, and the best way to perfect their art is to fully align in meditation with their guides,and the reason to endeavour to be at one with your guides is that they do all the healing work. You are merely a conduit to extend their energy which holds us in perfect wellness. They will know exactly what is required for the person who is being healed and will be using the healer's body as a conductor to allow the energy to flow into the person asking for healing.

I may add that you can do this for yourself as well if you can train yourself to accept whatever illness you have and ask to be shown how you may link with your guide to attune to that wellness.

So, to answer how healing works, we are energy encased in the physical, so all healing is done through divine unconditional love, which is pure, positive energy in perfect alignment with wellness.

- The master healers in spirit work with the healer to flow their energies through the physical body of the healers into the physical bodies of the people needing to heal.
- The more aligned the healer, the more energy can course through him or her.
- When the healer is highly attuned (an example would be a master such as Jesus), he or she would have been able, because of his or her highly attuned ability, to see complete wholeness of the sick person and heal that person with his direct connection to the higher energies of spirit; the more healing can take place.

Healing Others

From the eyes and heart of spirit, everyone is perfect.

We often focus so much on the physicality of a person that it is all too easy to forget the essence of the soul that they are, but when you change how you think about someone, they feel it and, without realising, start to change in response to the energy they feel.

If you want to help heal someone, don't look for what's wrong with them, but hold them in a vison of wellness. Your ability to see them as healed is a vibration that they will subtly pick up on, and constantly holding a person in a vison of wellness and focusing on their strengths and qualities is the quickest way to help heal them and also to bridge any conflict you may be having.

- ❖ Be the best conductor of energy that you can be, and that means by working on your own instrument or body and attuning yourself through meditation.
- ❖ Clarify your thoughts first to align with perfect wellness.
- ❖ Hold someone in a vision of perfect wellness and allow your energy of wellness to flow through you.

Healing Yourself

A few years ago when I was feeling mentally and physically stressed one day, I decided to take a bath to relax. I did the *Golden Chair Meditation* listed below to help me feel less stressed and relive the aches and pains I had in my body.

What I will always remember is that when I opened my eyes after the meditation, the original clear water in my bath had turned aqua blue in colour!

I stared at the blue colour in disbelief for a few moments

and then it just faded away. At the time, I had no idea why it happened, but I know that we draw the colour to us that are most beneficial to heal us at the time. I needed the lighter blue to help me just relax.

I know I felt a whole lot better physically and mentally after that meditation experience, and the feeling of peace lasted all day!

I cannot say what your own personal experience will be, but I hope you find the healing waters of the Golden Chair Mediation helps you as much as it did me.

From the Angels to All Who Ask the Divine Realm This Day

Through thine eyes do we see the need for healing
and love. We are here to tell you we are with you;
you are not alone in your troubles or your pain.
Let go of all fear and listen to the voice
that whispers in your heart, you are loved
and you are one with the divine.
Let go of pain and sorrow and embrace
the moment you have right now.
Embrace the change that comes from being
free of fear and pain and embark on a new
journey, one of awe and wonder at the power of
the divine angels to sing their song of love, to
heal all hurts through unconditionally bringing
their presence and healing rays to you.
Know that angels hear your prayer.
Be at peace

Complete This Exercise

Start with the beginning of the breathing into peace meditation to relax you then carry straight on into the *Golden Chair Healing Meditation* without a break so they flow as one meditation.

Breathing into Peace Meditation

o   I want you to close your eyes and focus on your breathing. Breathe in deeply through your nose and out through your mouth three times.

o   Keep focusing on your breathing and as you inhale say in your mind:

- *This is my time. I allow myself to relax.*

o   Keep your focus on breathing deeply two more times and say:

- *I am powerful. I am at peace.*

Now follow immediately on with the Golden Chair Meditation without stopping.

The Golden Chair Meditation

o   Send out your thoughts of love and appreciation for the present moment and breathing deeply once more ask your twin-soul angel to join you.

o   Feel their loving presence around you, reassuring you that all is well.

o   As you walk together a shimmering waterfall glistens and sparkles in front of you. You can see through into a tranquil oasis of colours and sounds as you walk through.

o   There is a crystal-clear pool of water ahead that you both decide to sit next to.

o   Listen to the harmony of the water. Its music is calming, making you feel peaceful and relaxed.

o   Place your hand into the water and feel the colours of the water come alive, blending with you as they change with your every movement.

o   There is a golden seat in the pool. This is your seat. Step into the pool and gently relax into the golden seat.

o   You feel instantly at ease and happy under your angel's protective gaze as you allow the changing colours of the water to drift over your body as you sit in your golden seat.

o   You can feel your feet on the ground as the warm water of the pool moves with your body.

o   Feel the harmony of the water merging as one with you as the colours seep into every fibre of your being.

o   Watch as a light shines up from below, changing the water into a single colour. Notice the brightness of the colour you are immersed in.

o   Feel the healing and wellness lift you as you become weightless in the light of the colour.

o   At one with the healing in this moment, you are perfectly well and whole and full of vibrancy, as every very limb of your body feels alive, illuminated by the life force of the healing pool.

o   Full of vitality and glowing with energy, allow yourself to drift within this peaceful moment of oneness.

o   There is nothing for you to do or be in this moment as relief fills your heart full of love and appreciation for your wellness.

o   Completely at peace within the energised feeling of your whole body, gently drift back and relax into your golden chair.

o   You can see your twin-soul angel standing next to the pool, and you step out of your golden chair and out of the water to greet the angel again.

o   You walk in complete harmony together back through the waterfall.

o   Waving goodbye to your angel, once more allow yourself to feel the joy of your deeply relaxed body as you breathe into full contentment of the moment, coming back into your peaceful space and opening your eyes.

Chapter 23

LEARNING TO CHANNEL

Learning to channel is all about your specific intention. I asked for answers and help when I first began channelling, and I wasn't sure where the words were coming from but I just kept going. Anything you do in life is trial and error. You fall off your proverbial bike many times as you reach for the experience of riding until you can ride with ease. So as a child learns about life in the physical, learning all the new experiences from birth, walking, talking, and awakening to who they are, so you then become aware you are starting from the beginning and learning to reconnect to source.

To be a conscious channel is to connect with your guides and allow their unconditional love and wisdom to flow through you.

Your guides are a droplet of the sea of oneness, as you are, but they are focused in divine conscious, God or divine intelligence. They then communicate with you in your physical form, from their focus in the divine, spiritual, or God consciousness. It is, therefore, a two-way process of communication from your guides broader more expansive focus in divinity to your narrower focus in the physical.

There are two main types of channelling or communication with your guides.

Unconscious Channel

If you are an unconscious channel, it will be like falling asleep. In a deep meditative state, your conscious awareness disappears, and you are unaware of your guide's message or words as they work though you. When you are an unconscious channel you do not remember anything your guides have said when you come back into your conscious mind.

Conscious Channel

If you are a conscious channel, you will be able to remember or be aware of some of your guide's words or messages but not all of them.

I am a conscious channel. I have always been able to stay awake and be conscious of my guides words as they spoke through me. I can hear internally or sense the energy of what is being said by my guides.

Most often, I cannot remember what they have said an hour later! To give you some idea of what it is like, when I first started channelling, I felt as though I was talking to myself. I could hear my own voice inside my head, which added to my belief that it was me alone! I now know this to be the most effective way of your guides joining with you.

They do so very softly at first so you do not realise they are there, as a way of gently getting you used to their presences as they attune or align their vibrational energies with yours. Your guides overriding objective is to work with you in unconditional love. They will not do anything that may cause you concern.

As you progress and your vibration raises, your guides will start to deepen the connection so you can then differentiate between their words and your own.

Quite often, I have to go and look up the meaning of a word I have channelled, which, although a little bit frustrating, is a sign to me that it is my guide's words I am channelling.

As I progressed in daily channelling, I realised I would be writing something, and my mind would suddenly think about it, and as I did that I became aware of a *word battle* going on in my head as three different words with the same meaning would come up. By that, I mean that when I channel, I hear the words ahead of my writing. I can hear a whole sentence as I am still writing the previous words, as though I am taking dictation. So if I then think about what I am writing, my conscious mind adds to the words and, hence, the confusion of what to write. It can happen so fast that I can hear about ten words all at the same time diverging into different directions or sentences, as though I could write three sentences at once if I had more hands!

I realise now that I lost focus, and my guide would add words to follow on my thoughts, and I lost focus again, taking it in a different direction, and my guide would correct the direction by adding a different sentence. You can see how confused I became at first until I learned to focus.

I learned to focus by not thinking about what I was writing – not editing or looking at words. If I felt myself slipping, my guide would then pull back, I could feel my energy slow, and the words would feel wrong and the flow would stop.

Your guides will assist you in any endeavour that you are undertaking. As you practise attuning and meditating, your guides will start to close the gap in the vibrations and join into your energy fields until you are eventually merged as one with your guides.

When you have become adept at mediating and creating a balanced energy field that your guides are used to merging with you, they will then automatically start to work through you.

It has taken me many years to become consciously aware of my guides as they work though me. It may not take you that long, as everyone is different, but be prepared to dedicate your time to meditation if you want to achieve this level of mastery at allowing your guides' energies to flow through you so you are recognise their input in your daily life.

Conscious Channelling

How Do You Tell Your Guides' Presences from Imagination?

This can be difficult at first but the hallmark of your guides are the following:

- ❖ The feeling of pure unconditional love they come with
- ❖ The speed of the communication (very fast)
- ❖ The feeling of being uplifted long after the message
- ❖ The impression of the message staying with you, easily and clearly recalled long after the event
- ❖ The lack of being commanded to do something as opposed to always being guided in love

My guide's signature statement to me when I am struggling with something and I ask for help is "it would be better if." Learn to discern spiritual communication by the feeling to begin with.

Your guide's presence will be an overwhelming feeling of love and well-being that you will feel uplifted by. That is the hallmark of a true, high-vibrational guide, the feeling of love as they draw close to you. They will guide and support you thorough any difficult times, and it will always be a positive experience.

You may find that you are a good communicator at speaking your guide's words also. If you want to try that out, then ask a trusted friend to sit with you as you start to channel, and get the friend to ask a few simple questions as you start to channel your guide.

When I first started speaking though my guide, my voice changed a little. It was slower and a little deeper until I got used to my guide, and then I went back to my normal voice, but the tone was still my guide. Whatever you feel most comfortable with will start to become clear as you practise your channelling.

I said at the beginning of *Blooming into Consciousness*

that I had no intention of writing a book. I was just channelling to gain help in my own life. That's a good way to approach channelling, by purely asking for help with your own concerns. It is not selfish to ask for your own needs to be met. The stronger you are in our own understanding and connection, the easier it is for you to help others.

Once you become comfortable with meditating and aligning your vibration into a calm state of allowing with your guide, you can more easily move into conscious channelling.

I said earlier it is about intention, and that is the most important part of the start of your channelling.

To be clear here, we have talked before about meditation and alignment to help you manage your daily life to bring about the things you desire, but to be a conscious channel and connect consciously with your guide is to help you in understanding the purpose and meaning in your life here, now, in the physical.

Whether it is a relationship, health, or wealth that you seek or have achieved, at some stage it will not be enough. Your desire to understand past the physical and reconnect to source is the strongest desire you will ever have. It will never leave you, as you are source, and you feel the constant calling home of your energy as a reminder of the unconditional love that supports you as you navigate the physical. And the more you evolve, the stronger the call gets.

Always remember you are loved unconditionally and everything you do is always perfect in the eyes of the spirit world.

Complete This Exercise

Connecting with Your Guide – Circuit Meditation

- ❖ Close your eyes and focus only on your breathing.
- ❖ Breathe deeply and steadily until you are completely relaxed.
- ❖ Feel the weight of your body sinking into your chair as you let all the tension in your body drift away.
- ❖ Become aware when you breathe how the air fills your lungs to capacity before you release it.
- ❖ As you breathe out, notice the stillness as though time has stopped momentarily.
- ❖ Breathe in deeply and focus on your third eye in the middle of your forehead.
- ❖ Ask your guides to let you know they are with you.
- ❖ You may only feel a light sensation, as though knowing without seeing their presence.
- ❖ Now move your focus to the top of your head.
- ❖ Feel the top of your head become open as though it was filling with a beam of light shooting up and touching the stars.
- ❖ Now follow the light back down through the top and back of your head and feel it move all the way down the back of your spine.
- ❖ You may feel your spine tingling like an electric current as the energy travels through you.
- ❖ Feel the energy moving down your spine, then move underneath your seat and up through the front of your body, through into your chest

area, and then up through the front of the top of your head, and back up to the stars completing a circuit.

❖ Breathe in and follow the circuit up from you head to the stars, down your spine, under your seat, and through your chest into your head and back up.

❖ Notice any changes in your body such as your breathing changing. You may see, sense, or feel movement within your body.

❖ Breathe, relax, and allow yourself to be in this flow of spiritual energy in the circuit.

❖ Now thank your guides for drawing close to you and feel their energy lifting away from you.

❖ Notice your body feeling heavy in your chair once more.

❖ Feel the weight of your limbs as you wiggle your fingers and toes as you move back and become present as you open your eyes and come back into the room.

Complete the *Connecting with your Guide – Circuit Meditation* and then follow straight on with the exercise below.

• Have a pen and paper or pad ready for you to write down the words you are going to channel.

• Make your intention to connect with your guides and do not focus on how it will flow or if it even makes sense.

Complete This Exercise

Aligning with Your Guide to Write

- ❖ In your calm state after your *Circuit Meditation*, breathe deeply in and out for a short while, then pick up your pen and paper.
- ❖ Ask a question and then just start to write.
- ❖ You could ask for your guides' names or what they look like or the style of clothes they are wearing, or you might simply be asking for help with a situation in your life.
- ❖ It's important not to edit or read what you have written until you have finished. Even if you write a whole page of nonsense, it doesn't matter. The whole page is a tuning exercise where your guides are lowering their vibrations a little and raising yours to meet them.
- ❖ It will take time to align, and practising is the only answer until eventually you will start noticing a difference in how you write.
- ❖ The tone of what you are writing will start to change a little and by that I mean it will not be how you would normally phrase certain words.
- ❖ You will find you are writing faster as the connection develops and you move into your guide's vibrational field. There will also be a knowing and a wisdom behind the words that flows effortlessly.
- ❖ The most important thing to remember is there will be no negative comments or any bad feelings – everything that is given to you will be done in love.

A Final Word

Every part of my being is in full bloom

Go kindly with yourself and others. Speak
from the heart your own truth. Do not fear
retribution but instead move forward into the
promised land of hope, light and love.

You are not alone and never will be.

Be at peace and live well my
friends until we meet again

Namaste

Printed in the United States
By Bookmasters